SURVIVOR'S OBLIGATION

Navigating an Intentional Life

CHRIS STRICKLIN

JOEL NEEB

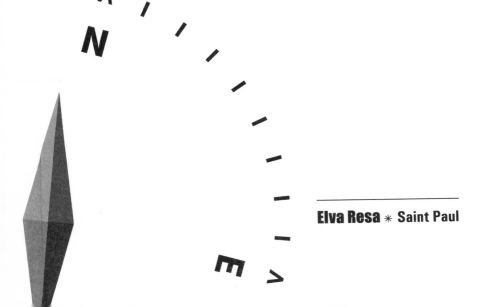

Elva Resa * Saint Paul

Events in this book are true. Some names have been changed.

Design by Andermax Studios. Front cover sky photo by Chris Stricklin. Compass by Brenda Harris. Senior editor Terri Barnes.

Library of Congress Cataloging in Publication
Control Number: 2019016280
ISBN 978-1-934617-47-2 (hc)
ISBN 978-1-934617-49-6 (epub ebook)
ISBN 978-1-934617-50-2 (kindle ebook)

Printed in United States of America.
10 9 8 7 6 5 4 3 2 1

Published by
Elva Resa Publishing
8362 Tamarack Vlg., Ste. 119-106
St. Paul, MN 55125

ElvaResa.com
MilitaryFamilyBooks.com
Bulk discounts available.

For the survivor in all of us.

*For Terri: Our life continues to be an adventurous journey,
and together we savor the moments of each day. —Chris*

*For Marsha: You made our family's survival possible,
and every day after worth surviving for. —Joel*

Contents

Survivors

On September 14, 2003, Chris "Elroy" Stricklin ejected from his U.S. Air Force Thunderbirds F-16 fighter plane less than a second before it crashed to the ground and erupted into a massive explosion. He landed under his parachute not far from the wreckage of his aircraft.

Joel "Thor" Neeb was also an air force fighter pilot, but his greatest battle would not be in the air. In March 2010, he was diagnosed with stage IV cancer. His doctors gave him a 15 percent chance to live five years. At the same time, doctors also discovered a tumor in the lung of Joel's three-year-old son.

EACH OF OUR LIVES CHANGED in an instant. For Chris, it happened just before his aircraft hit the ground. For Joel, it was the moment he received a dire diagnosis. We both knew our chances of survival were slim, and we each made a choice. We chose to do all we could do to live. Later, we realized we would also have to choose a new way to live.

Although we both served in the air force, we first met after leaving active duty, as members of the same consulting firm. In a strategy session one day, we participated in a team-building exercise that involved creating a timeline graph of our lives. Positive experiences were high points on the timeline; negative experiences were low. We each placed our individual brush with death among the lowest points. Interestingly, for both of us, after the low points of our traumas, the lines of our lives marched upward in a steady trajectory. Our trials had become turning points, but we both had more healing to do.

When we met, we found comfort in connecting with another person who had come so close to death. It gave us freedom to talk about how our experiences had changed us. Chris survived an unsurvivable ejection and Joel survived an unsurvivable cancer. Experts said it was not probable for either of us to be alive, yet we are.

At first, our conversations with one another focused on the ways our experiences were different: We had survived completely different traumatic experiences. We also discovered similarities: We had each found answers in the questions, clarity in the fog, and a renewed hope for the future when we faced what we thought was the end of life.

During many phone conversations between us, one or the other has broken down in tears while sharing portions of his story. Unpacking the memories and emotions of these ordeals was more painful for each of us and our families than we had imagined.

Although it was a rocky emotional journey, we discovered healing in the process of writing about our experiences. Writing our stories forced us to come to terms with all the emotional weight these events held. It allowed each of us to open our hearts more fully to our spouses, engage in deeper conversations, and build stronger relationships.

We both know many airmen who did not walk away from a crash as Chris did. Many friends who fought battles with cancer, undergoing chemotherapy alongside Joel, did not receive the second chance Joel was given.

We didn't do anything special to deserve it, and yet we both survived.

People who survive near-death encounters sometimes have feelings of remorse—*survivor's guilt*—for living through an experience when others did not. Neither of us experience that guilt. Instead, we both feel compelled to work through the pain of reliving our experiences, to learn from them, and to live differently because of those experiences. Rather than remorse, we feel a *survivor's obligation*, a responsibility to live our lives in a new way—for ourselves, our families, and on behalf of those who did not get a second chance.

On Joel's seventh anniversary of being cancer free, Chris sent him this message: "There is an appreciation for each day, shared by people who almost lost tomorrow!"

While we have this in common, our near-death experiences revealed different truths to each of us.

After his ejection, Chris chose to focus on his family over his career. After his illness, Joel became determined to seek challenges and adventure alongside his family. For both of us, a survivor's obligation means making daily decisions based on our deeply held values.

Together, we also felt a desire to share our stories and how our experiences changed our perspective. Knowing what we hold dearest, we now live our lives intentionally and in the light of discovering what is most important to us. Instead of making decisions we can live with for today, we make decisions that reflect the values of a lifetime.

Elroy's Story

IT WAS A ROUTINE THURSDAY for me and the other members of the United States Air Force Air Demonstration Squadron, more commonly known as the Thunderbirds. We had an early morning brief at our home station at Nellis Air Force Base in Las Vegas, Nevada, for the day's flight to a show location in Reno, a short flight away on the other side of the state.

The day began like many others for our team, with a group of pilots in signature blue flight suits sitting around a conference table, briefing the details of the day's deployment sortie, which is what we call a flight. Our mission that day was to fly our aircraft to Reno, Nevada, to set up for a series of three performances over three days at the National Championship Air Races.

Every fighter pilot has a call sign, a name chosen for us by our fellow pilots. Mine is Elroy, because of my resemblance to the cartoon character in *The Jetsons*. In many cases, a call sign stays with a pilot for life. This changes temporarily when a pilot becomes part of the Thunderbirds team. Those chosen for the team serve a two-year stint, and during that time team members are known by a number indicating their position on the team. Thunderbird 1 is the squadron commander, Thunderbird 2 is the left wing, 3 is the right wing, 4 is the slot. These designations indicate the position in the Thunderbirds' four-ship formation called the Diamond. Thunderbird 5 is the lead solo. My position on the team was Thunderbird 6, the opposing solo. Other team members have number designations also, such as the narrator,

Thunderbird 8 (also a pilot) and the team doctor, Thunderbird 9.

After a flight to any show location and before landing, the six demonstration pilots fly a series of arrival maneuvers to check out ground reference points and practice some of the maneuvers for the air show. Then the team's maintenance personnel prepare the aircraft for the show, fueling them and checking systems for the next flight. After the pilots land their aircraft, the commander and two solo pilots board a helicopter for a survey flight to examine the timing points again from the air. This routine procedure at each new show site allows the team to examine the terrain, clarify timing points for the demonstration, and refine their ability for precision in the high-performance F-16 fighter aircraft. After the helicopter flight, the team reassembles and briefs the details of the demonstration show.

This is what we did when we flew into Reno—arrival maneuvers and a helicopter survey. My third flight of the day was the show performance for seventy-five thousand or so aviation enthusiasts at the air races.

The aerial portion of a Thunderbirds demonstration is approximately thirty minutes of close-proximity, high-speed precision flight. Following each demonstration, the team reassembles to debrief the performance and refine our skills for the next flight. In this debrief, we examined each maneuver in excruciating detail. We covered how to duplicate the movements we executed with precision and how to improve and refine those we did not.

After the final show at Reno on Saturday, maintenance prepared the aircraft for a cross-country flight to the next show location. The team calls this a show fly, when a show at one location is followed the same day by a flight to the next day's performance site. Our next destination was Mountain Home Air Force Base, Idaho.

When we arrived at Mountain Home AFB, all the demonstration aircraft were low on fuel. We accomplished a few of our arrival maneuvers, but because of our fuel levels we could not complete the entire arrival practice nor see all the ground timing points. Ground timing points are predetermined features on the ground used to calculate and correct the timing of the show.

For all Thunderbirds demonstrations, show center is the center of the show line, a predetermined point over which all maneuvers during the show are focused. The location of the show line provides optimum viewing by the spectators and, most importantly, a safe distance from the maneuvers, as determined by Federal Aviation Administration rules. This distance is adjusted depending on the particular maneuver of each fighter aircraft. For example, a jet flying straight and level is permitted to pass closer to spectators than an inverted or looping aircraft.

Our normal arrival maneuvers began with the Delta formation—a triangle formed by all six Thunderbirds—followed by the first four maneuvers of the planned show. For the other solo pilot and me, this included the Opposing Knife-Edge Pass. In this maneuver, the solo pilots begin eight miles apart and fly directly toward one another—reaching a closure airspeed of nearly fourteen hundred miles per hour—at one hundred feet above the ground. We synchronize this flight with analog stopwatches mounted to each of our dashboards.

At the first practice run at Mountain Home AFB, using the ticking of the second hands on our stopwatches, we maneuvered our aircraft toward predefined timing points. As we closed on show center, our speed brought the two aircraft a mile closer every three seconds. Twelve thousand feet from show center the lead solo, Thunderbird 5, called the maneuver, "Knife-Edge." To acknowledge the direction as opposing solo, I responded, "Knife-Edge." At the next checkpoint, Thunderbird 5 called, "Eight thousand, smoke." As the S in smoke was spoken, we each turned on our smoke. One second later, when both aircraft were six thousand feet from show center point, Thunderbird 5 called

"Six thousand," speaking S in six when his jet was precisely over the six-thousand-foot reference. Just over five seconds later, both aircraft approached show center, targeting the optical hit, the nanosecond we would meet directly over show center. As the final few feet of closure ticked away, I maneuvered my aircraft a few feet above Thunderbird 5 to ensure the look angle from the ground would give the appearance of the aircraft passing completely level. Then Thunderbird 5 called "Ready, hit it!" At this call, I ensured a fifty-foot separation between the trajectories of our two aircraft. As we met over show center—at the very last moment—we each snap-rolled our aircraft to ninety degrees of bank to avoid collision, passing a mere fifty feet apart.

For me, the next item on the arrival maneuvers script was the Inverted-to-Inverted Roll. For this maneuver, I entered the show line two miles from show center and flipped my aircraft, flying to show center upside down. Over the six-hundred-foot target window of show center, I performed an aileron roll—a full revolution about the aircraft's longitudinal axis—returning to an inverted flight position. While this looks like one of the simpler Thunderbirds maneuvers, any pilot knows the negative gravity it involves makes it tricky.

We walk around on this earth at the force of gravity, or 1 G, and a pilot in an aircraft flying straight and level experiences the same force. At that gravity force, a two-hundred-pound person weighs two hundred pounds, and the heart is able to efficiently pump blood through the body to supply oxygen to the brain. When a pilot maneuvers the aircraft into a turn, the acceleration and the force of gravity both increase. When the force reaches nine times the force of gravity, or 9 Gs, the same two-hundred-pound person weighs eighteen hundred pounds, and the heart has to work much harder to pump blood throughout the body. To help the heart keep blood flowing in a high G-force situation, pilots learn a specific technique, called the anti-G straining maneuver or AGSM, which uses breathing and isometric muscle contraction to counteract the forces on the body. The AGSM helps ensure oxygen is continuously transferred to the pilot's brain. Otherwise, the blood will pool in the lower extremities and the brain will be deprived of oxygen, causing loss of consciousness. To aid the AGSM, a fighter pilot wears a G-suit. The suit looks similar to cowboy chaps and contains air bladders that pressurize through a G-sensitive connection to the aircraft and press firmly on the pilot's legs and abdomen.

Positive G-forces are the easy part. When the aircraft is upside down, the gravitational force becomes negative. Instead of being pushed into the seat, the pilot is hanging in the straps, being pulled toward the ground and away from the seat. Instead of blood pooling in the lower extremities, it is now forced into the pilot's cranium, which can result in bloodshot eyes and a terrible headache. Negative Gs add to the difficulty of flying upside down. As a Thunderbirds solo pilot, I learned to love inverted flight because I spent a lot of time there.

At every show location, the Thunderbirds receive a detailed satellite photo to determine specific points for precise timing of each show. Thunderbirds 5 and 6, the solo pilots, share points six thousand, eight thousand, and twelve thousand feet along the show line to either side of show center, and a point thirty degrees behind the show line on each side, four miles away, where we begin our timing runs to meet precisely at show center. These are the points we use to coordinate maneuvers like Knife-Edge Pass and others that require exact precision.

The initial plan that day at Mountain Home was to verify our points, then practice our first few maneuvers. Mountain Home was a challenging location, one I had never flown before, and the points were difficult to determine. The satellite photo we received was taken from an angle, instead of directly overhead, invalidating the scale and making the photo data challenging to use. This caused significant problems with timing as well as precise point determination. We extended the flight survey in our F-16s to try to align the predetermined points. Although a critical step, it left us with less fuel than planned; neither I nor Thunderbird 5 had enough fuel to complete our practice maneuvers.

We landed at the base and took a routine helicopter flight so the three key pilots of the air show orchestration could survey at a slower airspeed, compare our opinions, and determine consistent points. Adjusting for the angled satellite photo increased the complexity. I returned with Thunderbird 5 to the briefing room to further discuss and refine our points.

Another Show

When I woke the next morning, September 14, 2003, and opened my eyes on an otherwise beautiful Sunday, I had a sinking feeling. Something was wrong in my world, but I could not put my finger on it. As I climbed out of the hotel bed, the apprehension I felt drove me to call my wife, Terri, to confirm everything was okay back in Las Vegas. She confirmed all was well with her and our two children, Zachary and Bethany. I couldn't understand this vague and unpleasant feeling. Thinking about the day I faced, I realized the last week had been a total whirlwind of travel. The show we performed only the day before at Reno already seemed part of the distant past. The flight to Idaho and our arrival at Mountain Home were a blur of action. It was the fiftieth anniversary year for the Thunderbirds, and it had been a busy and complex show season.

That morning, I rushed to get ready, as we were all directed to go in early. Normally on a show day, I would go for a run to clear my mind before our demonstration, but I didn't have enough time that day. Shortly after arriving at the briefing room, I sat with Thunderbird 7, the operations officer, who is also the safety observer, to discuss my anxiety for the day's performance. I recounted my concern over the show.

"Something's just not right," I said.

Of all my maneuvers for the show, Max Climb with Split S was the most difficult and had the least margin for error. It was also my takeoff maneuver, so it was one I did not practice during our arrival maneuvers the day before. As a result of my uneasy feeling, I requested to switch to my backup takeoff maneuver instead. Thunderbird 7 reminded me I was a skilled aviator chosen for my ability to fly the aircraft. Request denied.

As always, ninety minutes before flying, our team briefed the demonstration, proceeding through a deliberate pattern and well-rehearsed script to talk through each maneuver of the show. In the course of a season, the Thunderbirds team performs in many different locations, all with very different terrain. The team adjusts for those differences at each show, while keeping procedures as uniform and according to pattern as possible.

In the morning briefing, we again discussed the timing points for Mountain Home. We found out the angled satellite photo we'd used the day before to determine our timing points was completely inaccurate. This meant all the points we had determined the day before in our arrival maneuvers and confirmed on the helicopter survey flight were incorrect. Instead of the satellite photo, we would have to rely on a black-and-white schematic of the runway to triangulate new points with a new scale. It was the first time we could remember ever moving the points right before a show, and we knew our timing would be challenging. Once we resolved the points again, we proceeded through the brief, maneuver by maneuver, normal operations, abnormal operations, hazards, and so on, as we had so many times before.

As the brief concluded, we were all thinking about our points. The points are significant in the big scheme of demonstrations to keep the timing between the Diamond formation—Thunderbirds

1 through 4—and the two solo pilots. Those points were detailed on a timing sheet strapped to our legs over our G-suits.

The show narrator introduced the team, and as I climbed into the aircraft, I still had the same sinking feeling inside. I taxied my aircraft to the end of the runway for the final checks before we began the show. As always, the show opened with a radio retransmission over the public-address system, so the spectators could listen in. It began with a check-in of all six members of the flying demonstration team, starting with Thunderbird 1, who called out, "Thunderbirds Check." The rest of the flying team then responded with their numbers in sequence. Then Thunderbird 1 addressed the spectators, welcoming them to the show and thanking them for having us there.

After the check-in and welcome, Thunderbird 7 turned off the retransmit of the interflight communications. The Diamond released brakes. Thunderbird 5 and I started our stopwatches, hitting them simultaneously to synchronize our roll onto the runway. Once we had our aircraft aligned with the runway, Thunderbird 5 passed the engine run-up signal, while we checked our engine instruments at 80 percent power. After confirming all instruments indicated as prescribed, I passed Thunderbird 5 a thumbs up, and he responded with a thumbs up back to me. Precisely twenty-five seconds after the Diamond released brakes, Thunderbird 5 called, "Five on the roll." I hit the stopwatch again to time my takeoff exactly twenty-five seconds after him.

Seconds ticked away. I thought about my first maneuver.

The Max Climb with Split S was a delicate takeoff roll, as I had to keep the aircraft rolling down the runway well past the normal liftoff point to prepare for a vertical pull. I needed to take off closer to show center to arrive back at show center at the bottom of the loop. For this performance, show center had been moved farther down the runway to permit better spectator viewing. We'd had considerable discussion in the brief that morning about how to compensate for being so far back from show center and still maintain operations within the structural limits of the F-16. To compensate, when Thunderbird 5 rolled, we determined I would accomplish a high-speed taxi down the runway, transitioning about twelve hundred feet closer to show center.

At the twenty-five-second point, I called, "Six on the roll!" As the aircraft surged down the runway with the acceleration of a top-fuel dragster, I intently watched both the crowd and show center, gauging my compensation for the abnormal launch position. As I passed two hundred knots, one hand on the stick and one on the throttle, I surged the jet off the runway and continued the pull toward sixty degrees nose-high. Because this was a maximum performance takeoff, flown near the structural limits of the F-16, I had to make an intricate sequence of G-load changes to permit the safe retraction of the landing gear during the climb. As I passed the predetermined roll altitude, where I began the roll to inverted, I thought, *Wow, that happened quick. My internal clock must be off today.* I heard the voice of my instructor from my days of Thunderbirds training.

Always trust your numbers.

I double-checked the altimeter and confirmed my altitude was correct.

Roll.

Now the aircraft was inverted, and I was climbing, floating skyward toward the predetermined altitude to begin my over-the-top pull. Over the top, OTT, is the highest point attained in any looping maneuver. The world fell away above my head as the aircraft, still upside down, climbed skyward. As I approached the OTT altitude, I pulled on the control stick increasing the G-forces and beginning to maneuver the aircraft back toward the ground in the back half of the loop. One last check of the altimeter; I read the altitude displayed then recalled the altitude of the runway, subtracted one from the other and called, "Six on top, three five." In plain English, this means, "Thunderbird Six is on top of the Max Climb with Split S maneuver pulling into the vertical at thirty-five hundred feet above the runway."

As I keyed the microphone button to speak, I stretched my neck back hard, straining to see show center like a gymnast sighting a landing for a back flip. As the nose of the aircraft tracked across the blue sky and passed through the horizon to point at the ground, I assessed the show site with my peripheral vision, focused on my alignment on show center. The jet felt fine as I continued to pull the nose around the loop. Training taught me I was committed to completing the maneuver after the nose began to track below the horizon and point nose-down in the vertical. Past that point, I had learned there was not enough altitude to abort the maneuver without hitting the ground. Everything proceeded as it had in the hundreds of times I had flown the maneuver before, until the nose passed approximately fifty degrees nose-low.

Then I knew something was wrong.

Ejection

In my peripheral vision, I could see the horizon and assess my position in relation to it. I knew immediately I would not be able to complete the maneuver without impacting the ground. A calmness I had never experienced before settled throughout my entire body. At the same time, my years of air force training kicked in. I began to act automatically, performing according to the emergency procedures ingrained in my subconscious by my flight instructors.

Quick check of the engine. *Fine.*

Quick check of the gear. *Retracted as planned.*

I considered ejecting. *Too low and still flying inverted. No chance of survival.*

I elected to continue the maximum performance pull on the aircraft controls required by the looping maneuver. At the ninety degrees nose-low position, the aircraft was pointed straight down just over a thousand feet above the ground. With continued calmness, I realized impact with the ground was imminent. I knew I needed to eject. I also knew the chance of surviving ejection from that position was exponentially low, but I would have to try. As I began to reach for the ejection handle with my left hand, I looked out the top right of the glass canopy at the thousands of men, women, and children standing in the crowd. I could not risk hurting anyone by ejecting at this point.

I am not going to make it.

Knowing the spectators were on my right side and the airfield control tower was to my left, I rotated the aircraft to the left to ensure it tracked away from the crowd. This also used some horizontal distance to minimize vertical altitude lost, through what is known as a slice maneuver. I carefully aimed the flight path of my doomed aircraft halfway between the crowd and the tower, so the wreckage would roll between them after impact, minimizing the chance of injuring anyone on the ground.

I knew there was nothing I could do but pull the aircraft away from the ground at the maximum level. I continued to max-perform the aircraft as I had been trained to do, aware the lives of those around me depended on my actions. At this point, I experienced an extreme temporal illusion, a stress-induced distortion in the perception of time. Time seemed barely to move; seconds felt like hours. I thought of my training, my Thunderbirds solo instructor yelling at me on the Indian Springs, Nevada, practice range for aborting vertical aileron rolls.

"It did not feel right," I had said.

"Trust your numbers," he had demanded. "The Thunderbirds have been doing this for fifty years, and those numbers are more tested and proven than you or I can sense."

Trust your numbers.

In my mind, all the numbers were spot on for this maneuver.

I thought of my wife Terri, our children Zachary and Bethany. How would their lives change without me? I pictured Terri being told about the crash, watched her drop to the floor in tears. I saw the kids run in to see what was wrong. At ages eight and five, they would not understand why Dad would never come home again.

The ground was getting closer, the nose of the aircraft approaching the horizon on the backside of the loop. While it looked to onlookers and in photographs like the aircraft was level, it was actually descending at an excessive rate, essentially falling out of the sky. I checked the airfield control tower just off my left side and confirmed the aircraft should not tumble toward the few people watching from the outside walkway after impact. I looked back toward the spectators, once again, to ensure the aircraft would remain clear of the show line and secure their safety. The crowd was well off to the right now, no danger to them. It seemed I could see each of the people standing against the orange fence, scanning their faces one by one. They were watching with energetic anticipation of the airshow in front of them, unaware of the tragedy about to unfold in front of their eyes.

Everything was as controlled as possible.

I had flown this maneuver hundreds of times. My mind rewound through the execution on that day and played it alongside the last time I flew it, alongside home station maneuvers. It happened quicker this time than previously, but the numbers were on plan.

Check. Double-check.

I rechecked the gauges of the aircraft to ensure everything was on plan and confirmed it was perfect. It seemed I could freeze moments in my mind. I could rewind them, replay them, and examine every aspect of the situation from an outside view.

Again I thought of Terri. We had been high school sweet-hearts. After graduating nursing school, she jumped in a U-Haul and drove from Alabama to Colorado to support me as I chased my dream of becoming a fighter pilot. The air force soon moved us to Wichita Falls, Texas, where I attended Euro-NATO Joint Jet Pilot Training. Thirteen months after our wedding, Zachary was born. Terri took care of our newborn, always aware of the stress and demands of my pilot training. She routinely stayed in the second bedroom of our house on base, so our crying newborn wouldn't disturb my sleep. Her priority was to allow me to focus. So many sacrifices to help me succeed.

The nose of my aircraft was above the horizon now, but the sink rate was no less. The aircraft was still falling toward the earth. Ninety-five miles per hour straight down. My last chance to eject was quickly approaching.

I remembered Eglin Air Force Base, my first operational combat assignment. Terri was about to deliver our second child, Bethany. The day before my unit was to deploy to Iraq, she woke me and said it was time to go to the hospital. As the unit security manager, I held vital information for programming our aircraft for the trip. I had planned to go to work to hand off the information in the early morning hours. I asked Terri to wait for thirty minutes while I drove to the squadron classified area to make the hand-off. Now I thought of how I had left her at home, alone, in labor while I went to work. I made it back home in time to get her to the hospital—barely. Twelve minutes after we entered the hospital parking lot, we were holding our new baby daughter.

Thunderbirds solo pilots fly with full nose-down trim to give them an even greater level of control and precision of the aircraft. In this situation, I faced a serious drawback of flying with full nose-down trim: For safety's sake, the ejection handle should be pulled with both hands. Because of the nose-down trim, however, releasing the aircraft controls in my right hand would force the aircraft toward the ground even faster. I would have to continue to fly the aircraft as long as possible with my right hand and pull the ejection handle with my left.

My thoughts flashed to my first combat deployment in 1998. We had a toddler and a newborn. I thought of Terri dropping me off at the aircraft hangar. My military unit, the Sixtieth Fighter Squadron, the Fighting Crows, was headed to a classified location on the other side of the world. The length of our deployment was unknown as the nation anticipated war. My thoughts drifted to the mental stress she must have endured throughout my career as she surrendered hers to be a single mom in my absence.

Back to the cockpit. Both my experience and training confirmed I was well outside the design envelope, or safe ejection window, of the Advanced Concept Ejection Seat (ACES II) in which I sat. There was no guarantee of success and minimal chance of survival.

I put this aircraft in this position, and I have to stick with it. No matter what. I took this aircraft off the runway today, and it is my responsibility to bring it back.

I knew there was minimal chance of flying safely out of this situation without impacting the ground, but I made my final decision not to eject. The captain stays with his ship; a pilot stays with his aircraft. I would not eject. I would continue to pull the aircraft away from the ground no matter what happened. As the seconds crawled by, I began to sense ground rush through my peripheral vision, indicating the impending ground impact. I knew the aircraft was about to hit the ground. At this point, I recognized how calm I was, how clear my thought process was, and how much the training I had undergone prepared me for this situation. My thoughts turned from the impending doom of my aircraft to my bride. She devoted her life to me, my career, the air force, our country.

I can't leave her a widow without trying everything I can to survive. I can't do that to Terri. I owe it to her to try to live.

Smoke began to fill the cockpit. Everything seemed to be in incredibly slow motion, as the canopy gently eased away from the dashboard and slowly separated from the aircraft. In real time, it took less than one tenth of a second. I watched uncomprehendingly as the canopy gently lifted off the aircraft. It seemed to take an hour.

How can this be happening? Why was the canopy jettisoning off my aircraft?

This would only result from me jettisoning the canopy or ejecting. A quick glance at the canopy jettison handle confirmed it was still in place and not initiated. Then I looked down at the ejection handle between my legs. Instead of its normal position against the seat, it was resting against my chest clutched firmly by my left hand.

My left hand.

The hand I had definitely instructed to stay on the throttle when I made the decision to stay with the aircraft and not eject. It was as if my decision not to eject had been transmitted to my right hand, the one I now consider my fighter-pilot hand. My right hand continued to fly the aircraft as it was instructed and trained to do. But my decision had been overridden by my left hand, the one I now call my family hand.

I owe it to Terri to try to live.

Those words echoed in my head for what seemed like an eternity as I stared at my left hand securely holding the ejection handle against my chest, connected to the ACES II seat by a metal tether, which had initiated the violent ejection sequence.

The ejection sequence.

Training snapped me back to reality. In the ejection sequence, two-tenths of a second after the canopy departs the aircraft, rockets fire to propel the seat up the rails and away from the doomed aircraft. I realized my neck was bent forward to stare at the ejection handle, in a position guaranteed to break my neck as the seat rocketed upward at over forty times the force of gravity. Instinctively, I moved my body to the position drilled into me by nine years of training. I pushed my feet against the rudder pedals with all my force to secure my body firmly against the seat and thrust my helmet into the head rest. I took in every detail as the seat rockets fired and flames engulfed the cockpit. Burned in my memory is the vision of smoke gently and slowly rolling over the sides of the seat to engulf my legs. At the very last instant, I released the control stick and quickly slammed my right hand on top of my left, squeezing them together to keep my arms from being ripped from my body as I entered the airstream. I felt the surge of the seat rockets as the ejection seat was propelled up the rails, and I began to feel the wind on my face. The F-16 is designed with warning lights just under the glare shield. As the seat separated from the aircraft, I turned only my eyes down toward the head-up display. The excessive G-load and multiple hundreds-of-miles-per-hour wind blast forbade any other movement as my body was firmly pressed against the seat.

As the cockpit fell away beneath me, I noticed one of the aircraft warning lights, about the size of a quarter, break loose and begin to tumble toward me. I lost sight of the majestic aircraft as smoke from the rockets enveloped my body. The thirty-degree recline of the ACES II, intended to increase the G-force tolerance of fighter pilots, kept me from looking down toward the aircraft.

Next, I felt the opening shock of the parachute as it deployed from the seat, snapping it and me around with the force of hitting a brick wall. I knew from my training precisely 0.45 seconds had passed since the ejection was initiated, but it seemed like hours.

My world went black.

Alive

The next thing I knew, I was standing on the ground. I looked from side to side. It was a beautiful Sunday afternoon. The sky was amazingly clear. The sun shone bright. I felt the true joy of every high point of my life. Every good moment, every win, every positive and significant occurrence in my thirty-one years. A smile spread across my face and true contentment flowed through my veins.

Wait...Why am I standing here?

I remembered where I was: Mountain Home, Idaho. I felt my heart sink and could not catch my breath. Seconds ago, I was flying in a majestic Thunderbirds F-16, and now I stood on the ground. The realization hit me with the force of a sledgehammer.

I ejected!

Training is a powerful thing. Even though I was standing firmly on the ground, I began to execute the post-ejection checklist embedded in me: Canopy, Visor, Mask, Seat-kit, LPU, 4-line, Steer, Prepare, Land.

The first step after an ejection is to verify the presence of a good parachute. Full canopy with no line-over, no twists in risers. I looked up and saw nothing. No parachute canopy, no risers from the harness I was wearing, no silk cloth intended to be a pilot's last resort for survival. Jumping with a round parachute, like the one packed in aircraft ejection systems, results in an extremely hard ground impact. This forceful impact requires a parachute landing fall, to dissipate the impact across multiple points of the body. It is a technique parachutists learn by jumping off a platform into a gravel pit, learning to thrust their bodies sideways as soon as their feet touch the ground, to distribute the landing shock sequentially along five points of body contact with the ground: balls of the feet, side of the calf, then thigh to hip and finally roll onto the back. A safe roll out of a high impact situation.

But I saw no parachute.

I am standing on the ground without a speck of dirt on my bright red show suit. Not possible.

Well, this is it. I am dead. This is what it is like in the afterlife.

With the same calmness I'd experienced a few seconds before in the aircraft, I began to look around. Always a spiritual person, I believed a light would lead me to the other side after death. Nothing.

I looked down at my custom-fit Thunderbirds boots and began to shake my head in disbelief. No light leading me to the other side. After what seemed like hours, I saw my parachute collapse to the ground in front of me.

Wait, I have a parachute! I must be alive!

I immediately cupped my hands to my face, as if to see if I was truly still alive. When I pulled them away, my hands were covered in blood.

Wow, I must have done severe damage to my face. But, I am alive.

My parachute canopy kissed the ground and then, reinflated by ground wind, tugged me forward. Automatically, I reached up to my chest and began to disconnect the quick-release connectors on the parachute harness binding me to the canopy. The left connector popped open as planned, but the parachute was blowing in the wind and pulling me with more force than I could counter. All the tension from the inflated canopy was surging through the right side, a cross connector strap ensuring the canopy remained inflated. Plan B. I popped the chest and leg straps of the harness and stepped out of it. With no weight to pull against, the canopy collapsed to the ground.

A new excitement filled my body.

I'm still alive!

I scanned the area. *No F-16. No fire. No smoke.*

My thoughts turned to my teammates. I looked to the sky and counted five Thunderbirds airborne in the skyline. Probably worried about me and what they just saw. Next I scanned the front of the crowd for Thunderbird 7, our safety observer. I extended my arm, giving him an exaggerated wave, so he could tell the team I was okay.

Hmmm. He is less than a half mile away, probably easiest if I just walk over to him.

I started to walk, but as I took my third step toward the show line, again my training kicked in, reminding me of the severity of my situation. All pilots are trained to expect a severe state of shock after ejection, to recognize the symptoms and how to react.

I looked around. *Beautiful day, clear and hot. No fire. No aircraft wreckage.*

Not possible.

Half my brain demanded I walk over to the safety observer, and the other half begged me not to move. Fortunately, training won out. I realized the burning wreckage of my F-16 must be somewhere very near me, but the state of shock induced by my ejection prevented me from seeing it. Carefully, I backtracked the three steps I had taken from my original landing spot. Knowing any movement might put me into a fire I could not see, I lay down. I consciously chose to lie in the spot where I landed. I lay there on my back waiting for someone to come get me. I stared up at the clear blue sky and thought about life for what seemed like an eternity. Finally, I heard a pickup truck slide to a stop in the loose dirt of the runway infield.

The flash fire of the jet fuel that had been burning all around me had burned out, as the aircraft tumbled away and continued to burn. I heard the sounds of someone climbing out of the truck and sprinting to me. It was the base fire chief. He leaned over me and we locked eyes.

"I am glad to see you," I said, looking up at his smiling face.

"Not near as happy as I am to see you," he replied, "Now, let's get you out of here."

An ambulance crossed the disturbed earth to arrive at my side. The paramedics secured a neck immobilizer and strapped me on a back board, reassuring me they had me now. When I was settled inside the ambulance, and the vehicle began to drive across the uneven dirt, I felt pain for the first time. My entire spine felt as if it were shattered to pieces. My eyes darted to the ambulance technician who was skillfully putting an IV in my arm in spite of the movement of the ambulance.

"I have two questions for you," I said. "First, did anyone get hurt?"

He looked at me, the neck brace, and the board immobilizing my entire body and replied, "Just you."

"And could I have made it and completed the maneuver without hitting the ground?"

Shaking his head with confidence, the young airman replied, "You made the right decision, sir. That aircraft was hitting the ground no matter what, with or without you, and we are glad it was without you."

The first responders riding in the ambulance with me were amazed at the impossibilities. The impossibility of surviving an out-of-the-envelope ejection. The impossibility of my landing in any portion of the fireball of the explosion and not being burned. I had been saved from the fire by the twenty-two-pound survival kit tethered to me through the ejection seat system. It impacted the ground before me, spraying fine granules of dirt and extinguishing the fire in an approximate ten-foot circle where I landed. An incredible chain of events enabled me to be lying on a backboard talking to them.

The paramedic team sprinted into the hospital, pushing my

gurney at top speed as the finest doctors in the air force began analyzing me from head to toe. It seemed as if thirty people all worked on a different part of my anatomy at the same time.

Someone kept poking needles in my right foot.

I finally said loudly, "Stop poking needles in my foot! I assume you are asking me if I can feel that, and yes I can, but with all the commotion in here I cannot hear you asking me, and it hurts."

After what seemed like another eternity, the lead doctor informed the room of professionals that they were spinning up the helicopter to transfer me to a trauma center in Boise. The initial diagnoses of my condition were a broken back and cardiac injury. The doctors thought the force of the ejection and impact of the landing may have ripped my heart out of place.

It would be a few minutes until we were in the helicopter.

Thunderbird 9 is the team's flight surgeon. Ours at the time was Dave Steinhiser, who happened to be my close friend and a classmate from the U.S. Air Force Academy. I asked to talk to him, because I knew he would give me an honest opinion of the situation and provide comforting, familiar support. He did not let me down when he arrived.

In another moment, Thunderbird 1 entered the room. He told me Terri had been notified about the crash by telephone before anyone knew my condition.

Back in our living room on Spotted Pony Drive that Sunday afternoon, Terri and the kids were watching *Jumanji*. She had looked at the clock at the usual Thunderbirds demonstration start time and knew I was flying the majestic red, white, and blue F-16 I loved so dearly. A few minutes later, the phone rang. She answered in the kitchen.

Military spouses live with the fear of an official car stopping in front of their house, of individuals in Class A service dress uniforms getting out of the car and knocking on the door. This is how the military informs a family their service member has died.

Fearing the incident would show up on the national news, and Terri would see it before someone could officially inform her, Thunderbird 1 directed Thunderbird 8 to call Terri on the phone. The commander gave the order mere seconds after the event, while he was airborne over the fireball with no sight of me or knowledge of my condition. Dan "Danno" Carlson was Thunderbird 8 at the time. He did as a professional military member is trained to do. He executed the orders of his commander and made the call while someone else was on their way to our home.

This is the way Terri remembers the conversation.

"Hello."

"Terri, it's Danno."

"Hi, Danno."

"Terri, there's been an accident."

"Danno, did Chris wreck his rental car on the way to the show today?"

"No, Terri, there has been an aircraft accident and we don't know if he is okay ..."

Terri didn't hear any more. She dropped the phone and fell to the floor, sobbing uncontrollably, believing she had lost her high school sweetheart, her husband, the father of her children, her best friend. As the wife of a fighter pilot, she was confident this phone call meant a chaplain and another officer would soon arrive at our house to deliver the official notification of my death. Whatever was actually said on the phone line, that is what her heart heard.

Back in the emergency room, I was surrounded by people asking if there was anything I needed or wanted while we waited for the helicopter to arrive. Without hesitation, I told them I needed to call my wife. I knew she had been told about the accident, and she needed to hear my voice as proof I had survived.

No one in the room could get a signal on a cellphone. After

my crash in front of thousands of people, the phone systems were overwhelmed.

"I got you, sir," said an airman who appeared to be about eighteen years old. He picked up the landline phone and spoke authoritatively to the operator, "I need an emergency break through." Then the youngest and most innovative person in the room handed me an open phone line to connect with my wife.

Terri answered, and I heard the tears pouring from her heart through the line.

"Hey, Babe, it's me. I just wanted you to know I'm okay."

The rest of this phone call continues to be a point of disagreement to this day in our house. As I remember it, Terri began to yell at me like she never has before, screaming questions about what happened, why it happened, how happy she was I was alive. I could not get a word in between her questions.

With the helicopter ready for me to be boarded to lift off for the trauma center, I began to speak over Terri, who was still peppering me with questions and not allowing me time to answer.

"Baby, I know you are just reacting to the emotion of today. I love you, I will be okay. Now I have to hang up to take a helicopter flight."

For the record, Terri's recollection of the call does not include her yelling at me.

As the medical personnel began to load me on the medevac helicopter, the pilot came to speak with me and reassure me. The backboard was loaded very close to the roof of the helicopter, so as the rotors began to dig in for liftoff, all I saw was the ceiling. I began to think of the day's events, and of my wife and kids, their thoughts of my death, and how close they truly were to being without a husband and father.

Within minutes, the helicopter gently landed on the helipad in Boise, and it seemed as if a hundred people were waiting to catch us.

In a full sprint, they rolled the gurney to the receiving room and began working with determination and precision. They ran almost every test known to modern medicine to evaluate the spectrum of injuries: a suspected broken back, dislocated ribs, and more.

The two lead doctors stepped to the other side of the curtain surrounding me to discuss the situation. I heard one of them quietly say, "I can't determine why blood is pouring out his ears."

I quickly responded, "Hey doctors, this is not a soundproof room. You're only standing two feet away. Please step back in here to discuss with me the blood pouring out of my ears."

I couldn't reach up and check my ears or the blood flow, because my arms were still bound to the backboard.

Realizing I was conscious and lucid, the doctors discussed their initial suspicions of the damage to my body. None of it sounded good. Then they left. After an x-ray, MRI, and an alphabet soup of other machines and tests, I was finally alone, awaiting results of the tests. Wires and monitors were everywhere, seemingly connected to every part of my body.

Suddenly my heart began to race. Alarms sounded. A nurse ran in and hit another alarm to bring the team back together quickly. She leaned over me and asked, "What happened? Your heart is racing out of control."

"I just realized I ejected from my aircraft!" I said, anxiety gripping me as the events of the day hit home. The team worked to get my heart rate back under control. Apparently, the adrenaline that helped me survive the crash had just worn off. The period of heightened senses, increased strength, and minimal pain ended abruptly.

At one o'clock the next morning, a doctor walked into my room. It had been approximately ten hours since my aircraft hit the ground, and I had spent that time in a neck brace, strapped to a backboard, wondering if I would ever walk again and what level of brain damage I had sustained.

The doctor unstrapped me and said, "I recommend you do this slowly, but you can get up."

I stared at him for confirmation of what I just heard, and he explained the results of the tests. Something like thirteen of my twenty-four presacral vertebrae dislocated, three ribs dislocated, legs heavily bruised from opening shock. Nothing broken. He shook his head in disbelief and reminded me of the impossibility of survival at all, especially with no major damage.

A short time later I was released, and I walked out of the trauma center.

An air force flight surgeon who had accompanied me to the trauma center drove me back to the base. At approximately three in the morning, we pulled into the hotel parking lot at Mountain Home AFB. When we arrived, all the Thunderbirds were standing outside, clapping and cheering. It was like the atmosphere in a stadium after a sports player rises and walks off the field after an injury. Seeing all my teammates there to welcome me meant more than I can say.

I didn't rest much that night. I was in too much pain. When I left the hospital, I refused medication—no painkillers or sleep aids. At the time, I did not believe in pharmaceutically masking pain.

Morning arrived quickly, even with no sleep. It was surreal: a blur of events from ejection to medevac to "You're okay to walk out of here." I needed to know I was alive. I'm an early riser, and sunrise is my favorite time of day. It's a time when the air is crisp, clean, and new, and the sun reveals a new day, a new blank canvas.

Alone, I ventured outside, walking away from the buildings and into the massive openness of the Idaho landscape. I looked toward the impact site and watched with amazement as the sun peeked over the horizon, silently confirming I was truly alive to see another day. I took a single picture, because I knew this was a moment I would think back on for the rest of my days.

Critical Error

For the initial part of the safety investigation after the crash, I had to remain in Idaho a few days, so Terri flew out to be with me. As she ran to me, we embraced in what we consider the greatest hug ever known to mankind. For the first time since the phone call, she could actually feel I was alive. For the first time since the call, I could hold her as if to say how sorry I was for the stresses our military life had put on her, for the years she was a single mom while I was in combat, for the times she had picked up everything we owned and moved around the world to pursue a dream—my dream. For almost leaving her a widow. After our hug, I pulled away. Something was off, and we both knew it. I asked Terri to take me to the hospital at Mountain Home.

I struggled through the pain to walk into the flight surgeon's office and asked them to measure my height, which they had not done before.

I stood with my back to the wall, and the medical technician measured my height at five feet, eight inches. Opening my medical record to annotate the information, the tech saw the record of my height for the last nine years of my military service, a consistent five feet, ten and a half inches.

Two and a half inches shorter from the ejection. And it took a hug from my wife to know. She has always been a little shorter than me, and after sixteen years of hugging each other, we were used to where our faces met. Our first hug after the ejection told us something was different: my height.

In the following months, the doctors said they didn't believe my height loss could be a result of the ejection, a force estimated to be forty times the force of gravity, 40 Gs, as a pilot is thrust out of the cockpit on the rockets of the ejection system. They said it was more likely caused by the impact when I came back to earth. I landed on my feet and stayed on my feet after an impact equivalent to jumping off the roof of a three-story building.

The impossibility of this degree of compression without resulting fractures attracted many military specialists, all wanting to study my new height. Each one assured me, in their opinion, it was impossible for a person to lose so much height, because there is not enough cartilage in the human body to allow that much compression.

Each time, my reply was the same: "Doc, I understand your opinion on the impossibility of this situation, but the fact remains I am two and a half inches shorter."

When Terri and I boarded the flight to leave Idaho and return to Nevada, we did not realize we were subconsciously leaving the situation behind us. We never sat down and talked about what happened, never talked through the emotions of the events. For many years, we would not realize that as I pulled the ejection handle and physically shed my aircraft, I also let go of the identity that had defined my entire adult life. Up until that point, being a fighter pilot was the most important part of my life and my identity. But in the moments before impact, I was forced to decide between my professional identity and my family. The decision would change my life and priorities forever. Over a chocolate ice cream cone in the airport, without realizing it, Terri and I made the tacit decision not to talk about the Mountain Home event.

We returned to Nellis AFB, and I resumed flying F-16s but not with the Thunderbirds. I was assigned to the Sixty-fourth Aggressor Squadron. Like a cowboy getting back on his horse, I was drawn to return to the skies where I had always found comfort.

But something was different. In the previous nine years, I hungered to climb the ladder of a frontline fighter aircraft and get airborne. That hunger was replaced with anxiety the night before each flight. I shrugged it off as a leftover from the ejection incident.

Based on this anxiety and some good advice, I traded an assignment flying an F-15C at Kadena Air Base, Japan, for a tour at the Pentagon. Turns out, it was a much-needed break for the Stricklin family from the fast-paced world of fighter aircraft. After a few more months at Nellis AFB, our family moved to Washington, DC.

The results of the crash investigation were published soon after our move. After any aircraft crash, the air force conducts an exhaustive investigation to determine the cause or causes. Human error is among the causes of nearly all aviation accidents, and the sequence of events at Mountain Home would prove no different. My crash was determined to be the result of pilot error, more specifically, an altitude misinterpretation which permitted maneuver entry without enough altitude to complete the maneuver. The air force investigation went deeper to determine the root causes and factors substantially contributing to my error. Among other factors, they looked at squadron culture, training, pilot fatigue, and established safety margins.

Since the crash was the result of my actions, it helps me to understand what led up to those actions—and why my brain and my numbers told me the maneuver should have been perfect.

Our schedule had been crazy the week of the incident. We had limited fuel for arrival practice at Mountain Home, satellite problems with our pre-mission photos, timing points changed in the pre-brief, and my takeoff roll was unusually long. Most of us had considered this the most difficult show site of the season.

The question resonating in my mind was: How could I think I flew a perfect maneuver and end up standing on scorched earth? The answer was detailed by the investigation board president in this statement:

"There is evidence that three factors substantially contributed to creating the prospect for such a critical error: (1) The requirement for demonstration pilots to real-time convert MSL (Mean Sea Level) to AGL (Above Ground Level) numbers; (2) a maneuver with a limited margin for error; and (3) a preconscious level of awareness."

The investigator's third point best explained it to me: a preconscious level of awareness—describing unconscious but not repressed thoughts, which are therefore available for easy recall. For instance, I have often arrived at home after a hard day of work and realized I drove the path out of habit, without remembering the details of the trip. A preconscious level of awareness, my familiarity with the routine drive, allows me to drive home almost without thinking about it.

With the frustration, concern, and worry of our team that day, our commander had tried to settle down everyone with one small statement at the end of the brief: fly the show as if we were at home. Although the home practice range at Indian Springs was the same altitude as the runway at Mountain Home, the particular runway where I routinely practiced the Max Climb with Split S was at nearby Nellis AFB, a runway a thousand feet lower. So my autopilot numbers were off.

As a result of my crash and the investigation, some of the Thunderbirds show demonstration procedures were changed, including how the team converts real-time altitude numbers and calls them out during a show. Additionally, the altitude for the Max Climb with Split S was raised by one thousand feet, and overall safety margins were increased.

Regardless of how many "factors substantially contributed to creating the prospect for such a critical error," in the words of the investigation report it was my hand at the controls. I had narrowly escaped with my life, and my error was the ultimate cause. Initially, this was the hardest thing for my perfectionist mind to accept.

I would like to be able to say definitively how I dealt with this reality. I'd like to be able to say that expert statements describing it as a "perfectly executed ejection" make it easier. I cannot. The overarching truth is that I struggle every day with harrowing thoughts of *what if* and recurrent fears of *almost*.

In the aftermath of the incident, Terri and I did not talk about the crash. We avoided discussing how the tragedy—even one so narrowly averted—could affect us every day. We went back to life as usual, as much as possible, and began planning to add more children to our family.

During our next two duty stations at the Pentagon and in Turkey, we adopted two toddlers from China—a little girl Aubree Lu, when she was almost two; and a boy, Andrew, three and a half. With another daughter and son, our family was complete.

Every time I allowed myself to ask why I survived an unsurvivable ejection, to wonder if I accomplished what I was afforded a tomorrow to accomplish, Terri lovingly and gently replied, "We may never know, but it could be as simple as you surviving so we could adopt our two youngest children." Then she walked away to end the conversation. Otherwise, we never revisited those fateful minutes in the skies over Mountain Home. By not talking about it, we pushed it out of our minds, almost as if it never happened. I was aware of how I closed my mind to the crash.

When John Childs, a close friend, asked me about the crash, I told him I would never talk about it until my air force career was complete. Or so I thought.

Healing

For my next assignment, I entered requalification training to become an instructor for new fighter pilots at Columbus Air Force Base, Mississippi. Returning to flying fighters was hard for me, creating the highest anxiety level I had never known. Most nights before a flight I was unable to sleep. If I did sleep, I jolted awake, drenched in sweat. I felt like I could not talk to anyone about this without risking my flight status, my command opportunities, and my air force career. So I silently powered through requalification and became an instructor once again.

As I logged more time in the aircraft, I found sheer terror surged every time I donned my G-suit in preparation to walk to my aircraft. But I also found as I climbed the ladder to enter the cockpit, the anxiety stayed behind on the ground. I figured this meant I had it under control, and I vowed to not fly if my anxiety ever climbed into the cockpit with me.

This stress, anxiety, and fear continued during the four years we were stationed at Columbus AFB. I led a squadron of top military professionals who received recognition as the Top Fighter Training Squadron of 2012. No one knew the emotional pain it took for me to fly, and I felt truly alone, bearing invisible scars that turned my passion for flight into a recurring nightmare. After an assignment as a squadron commander, it's routine for rising air force leaders to go back to school for another master's degree. A year of school afforded me time out of the cockpit.

Within the next three years, I was promoted to colonel, served a ground combat tour just outside Kabul, Afghanistan, and spent ten months in a NATO assignment to the Centre of Excellence for the Defense Against Terrorism in Ankara, Turkey. These assignments all meant more time out of the cockpit.

Our family loved our time in Turkey, and our children agree it was the most educational and fun place they've ever lived. Growing up in a military family, our two oldest children took the lifestyle in stride, attending many different schools over the years. But we did not want to continue the same pattern with our two youngest children.

Terri and I cherish the opportunities air force life offered to two small-town Alabama kids. We lived in eighteen different houses over the course of twenty-three years. I had the opportunity to travel to thirty-five countries during my career, worked in the White House, the Pentagon, and deployed to classified locations the world over. But like many military families, we were tired. Tired of packing our lives in cardboard boxes and watching them drive away on eighteen-wheelers.

Friends assured me I would know when it was time to leave the air force, and Terri and I knew it was on the horizon. We agreed our next military duty station would be our last. My final assignment was Beale Air Force Base, California, which I requested instead of a possible assignment to an F-16 wing. I envisioned the sleepless nights and the anxiety flying fighters would cost me and decided it was not worth it. I wanted something less emotional, so I chose Beale. I thought flying the U-2, the T-38 trainer jets, and the Global Hawk remotely-piloted surveillance aircraft would be a more manageable level of anxiety than a combat tour in the F-16.

The U-2 soars at classified heights in what pilots call "low space," and flying in it requires a specialized flight suit designed for the environment. On my orientation flight, I saw the curvature of the earth and knew I was as high as any human except those in the space station. It was an amazing moment.

After being out of the cockpit for several years, I had to requalify to fly the T-38. Even though the T-38 is a smaller jet used for fighter training, flying it caused a resurgence of anxiety. I fought each day to hide my nightmares. But events were converging, conspiring to bring to light the pain I was trying to hide.

When we moved to Beale, I forged a close friendship with Dr. Paul Gourley, an osteopathic physician and the lead doctor in the Ninth Reconnaissance Wing. Severe back problems and pain are a residual reminder for me of the crash. I saw Paul routinely, when a vertebra would pop out of place, and I needed him to put it back through medical manipulation. Paul was a friend as well as my doctor, so we saw each other frequently, both in his office and in our neighborhood around the fire pit on our street. Paul knew me better than anyone else in the world besides Terri, and it turns out he knew me better than I knew myself. With his experience, expertise and caring, Paul saw evidence of the mental anguish I tried hard to hide. He allowed me to progress at my own pace as he helped me during this dark period. He routinely sat me down and asked how I was doing.

"What? Why? I'm fine!" was my routine fighter-pilot answer.

My friend John Childs was still encouraging me to bring my story to light. One day, John reached out to me with a question: "Remember when you told me you would not talk about your traumatic experience until you retired?"

I remembered, and I knew if I was going to talk to John about the crash, this emotional and significant conversation had to be in person.

John is also a medical professional and a longtime friend of mine and Terri's. He was in our wedding at the beginning of our air force journey. He and his wife, Amy, both Air Force Academy classmates of mine, had moved to San Antonio. So I flew there to see them.

Over a hamburger, I told John and Amy my entire ejection story from beginning to end for the first time, raw and unrehearsed. There were tears in all our eyes and pain in my heart. They knew telling my story could be meaningful to other people, as well as helpful to me, so John offered me an opportunity. He convinced me to deliver a keynote speech to a professional organization he belonged to, the Young Presidents' Organization.

We worked out a contract to include having Terri come with me for the presentation. I wanted her to be there, and I knew she needed to be there. I didn't realize her presence would be the hardest part of the event for her and for me, possibly one of the toughest challenges of our life. The event was scheduled a year out and would take place a few months before my official air force retirement. Plenty of time, I thought.

A few months later, I sat in front of my computer and began to develop the presentation that would lay bare my experience. Developing the outline was fairly easy. Putting the words and pictures to it was not. It took days, weeks, even months. Every time I ran the video of the traumatic event, every picture I saw, opened the memories. It brought back the trauma again in full force. Even though I had thought about the event every day since September 14, 2003, I had not embraced it, much less dealt with it. As a good warrior is taught to do, I had compartmentalized the details of the event out of my conscious memory. Dipping into those memories was like opening Pandora's Box. I began having problems sleeping. I became irritable, anxious, jumpy. I would wake up suddenly each morning in a cold sweat, not knowing why. At the same time, I was also fighting the anxiety of returning to flight in the T-38, and I continued to power through it.

Finally, the presentation came together. I thought the hardest part was over, but I began to realize how difficult it would be to tell the story with Terri there. I'm a passionate public speaker and love being in front of people. My military duties often entailed speaking in public, but I had a weakness. I could not talk about my family without tearing up. No matter what I did, my professionalism fell to the side when any thought or words came up about my wife and my family. About the Alabama girl who agreed to join me for a life of adventure in the military. We had always been all-in with each other.

I knew I had to ask Terri to listen to the story we had been keeping under wraps for so long. Once again, I was asking her to endure something for me, not for her. I had to be able to tell this story in front of a group with her present, without breaking down. Without being overcome with the emotions of what I put her through, what I put our children through, and what I had been through.

We can do this, I reassured myself as we sat in our living room and practiced the brief. Cue the first video, which opened with the internal radio communications of the Thunderbirds team that day in Idaho.

Five seconds in, Terri said, "I can't," and ran out of the room, and we both burst into tears. When the video began to play, she remembered the words she had heard thirteen years before.

Terri, there has been an aircraft accident and we don't know if he is okay...

We had not discussed the incident for all those years, because it was traumatic for both of us and our entire family. Even small things can trigger repressed memories and negative emotions. Terri and the kids were watching the movie *Jumanji* that Sunday afternoon when the call came in about the crash. If by chance the movie comes on the television, Terri simply says, "Turn it off," and I do. She cannot stand to hear any part of it.

Through the process of building a keynote presentation, I was asking Terri to dig up all those memories, to face those repressed feelings and address them head-on and in public.

"We have to get through this," I told her, knowing this was about more than a presentation. We made progress as I practiced with Terri listening. The first milestone was making it all the way through the videos without either of us breaking down. A month or so later, I made it all the way through my talk without tearing up too badly. Terri finally made it through the presentation, through the videos, the pictures, and the words, maintaining emotional composure. I thought we were making progress, but the journey ahead was longer than I realized.

While Terri and I were working on the presentation, we were reliving painful, repressed memories each evening, and I was pushing them away again each morning so I could go to work as a pilot. Paul didn't know about these conflicting stresses in my life, but he knew something was going on with his patient and friend.

After an episode with my back took me out of the cockpit for a short time, I went to Paul's office one day to receive the results of a flight waiver he was working on to return me to flight status. His eyes lit up as he proudly informed me the waiver had been approved, and I was cleared to get back in the air.

Poor Paul. I still remember the look on his face and the happiness in his eyes as he delivered what he thought was good news for me. His happiness didn't last. I started shouting at him, with no idea what I was saying, my frustration pouring off the leather couch where I sat. Paul met my anger with caring concern. He just sat there and listened, letting me vent the frustration I had saved for thirteen years. He absorbed my angst as I flung it at him. Repressed memories and feelings flew out of me, a combination of current anxiety and future worries about returning to combat flight status in a fighter aircraft. Paul's intent was to give me clearance to return to the T-38, but I heard him say I was cleared for a combat tour in the F-16. It was the last news I wanted to hear, yet I heard it.

My anger soon turned to pain, and I broke down. Paul said, "Chris, you know compartmentalizing this for thirteen years was not the correct way to deal with it. Let's work through this together."

Paul was my wingman, supporting me and challenging me both mentally and physically. He brought in a psychiatrist to aid my journey to recovery. I learned I had posttraumatic stress disorder, PTSD, as a result of the ejection. In therapy, I uncovered the repressed feelings and realized how my bottled-up emotions were manifested in more severe back problems. It was as if every memory brought with it another vertebra out of alignment, another knot in the muscles of my back, which already bore the physical injuries of the ejection.

Meanwhile, the date for the presentation arrived, and Terri and I traveled to San Antonio together for the event. As the time approached for me to take the podium, for the first time in my life I honestly thought I was going to pass out before going hot mike. It was time. Now or never.

Terri and I both made it through the presentation without a single memory sneaking out of our eyes and rolling down our cheeks. And for the first time, I told our story in public. It resonated with the audience. More importantly, it resonated in our hearts. Terri and I needed to share the most painful moment of our life together. It opened the door to memories we wanted to put behind us but needed to face. It forced us down the path of addressing the event and drew us closer together. For us, none of this was really about the event or the audience who came to hear my story. It was about Terri and me taking first steps toward healing and dealing with our story and our trauma.

But there was more healing needed and more to come. We had been avoiding this watershed event in our lives, and we had a lot of catching up to do. We had taken care of the visible wounds and tried to ignore the invisible ones. Silently and independently, we had suppressed our emotions, while I addressed only the physical ailments from the event.

Telling the story was the first step toward being open about our pain, but I had not told Terri everything. One step loomed on the path to recovery, one I was not ready to take: telling Terri about my emotional and mental suffering. We had talked about the crash while I was building the presentation, and we worked through the pain of the event, but only the event. Now I needed to tell her about the second- and third-order emotional effects. I did not want to admit I was suffering emotional problems from the incident, that I had been diagnosed with posttraumatic stress disorder. It felt like a weakness to me. I didn't want to admit it to her. I also didn't want to tell Terri I had been keeping a secret from her for thirteen years. Just the thought of discussing it with her brought me to tears. At every appointment with the psychiatrist, she asked me if I had talked to Terri. My reply was always the same: I had not found the right time. Paul asked me the same thing and urged me to talk to her about it. But I couldn't make myself take that step.

Until one Friday night. We were standing in the kitchen, getting ready for a family weekend of relaxation and fun. And it just flowed out.

"Terri, there is something I need to tell you."

She heard the tone of distress in my voice and gave me a familiar and comforting look.

"Terri, I have PTSD from the crash. I have been hiding it from you."

"I know," she said. "I sleep with you. Do you think I don't know why you wake up drenched in sweat? I didn't know you were hiding it, I just thought we didn't talk about it."

I looked at her in disbelief.

What? I stressed about this moment of revealing my feelings to her for months, and she knows?

She knew all along. She was experiencing her own issues from the event, which she had not shared with me. After that revelation, we began talking about everything, from my perspective and from hers.

Not long afterward, we closed the air force chapter of our life with military retirement and returned to Alabama, back where our journey began. After our years of travel, it was finally time to settle down to write the next chapters of our story.

We have learned that each chapter builds on the last and must take into account the wounds of the past, both visible and invisible. We don't try to hide them from each other anymore. Our relationship has always been close, but working through our individual struggles together has brought us closer. It's a process that is still going on and will continue throughout our lives together.

Each morning is a reminder of the way we choose to view our lives, a fresh start and a new day. As the sun peeks over the horizon, Terri and I sit on our patio, sipping our coffee. The sun's debut and the crisp, clean morning air confirm we are truly alive to see another day.

Another day to accept the events of the past and the ways they will shape our future.

Thor's Story

IT WAS JANUARY 25, 2010, my wife Marsha's thirtieth birthday. Our good friends, Jen and Whiskey, surprised us with a visit to our home in San Antonio, Texas, to celebrate with us.

When we began our careers together, flying F-15s, we were dubbed "Whiskey" and "Thor," call signs that would stick with us throughout our entire careers. I have never called Whiskey by his real first name, Jon, and he has never called me Joel. I don't know the true first names of many of the pilots I have flown with. The assignment of call signs is one of the fighter community distinctives no one outside our tight-knit profession really understands. To be honest, we like it that way.

Whiskey and I flew together first in Florida and then in Idaho. In 2010, he and his family were stationed in Virginia, where he flew the F-22. I was stationed at Randolph Air Force Base, where I taught new flight instructors to fly the air force's supersonic trainer jet, the T-38.

It had been quite a while since our families had been together, so I should have been having a great time celebrating Marsha's birthday weekend with close friends, but I was entirely distracted. The last few months had been crazy. In the previous year, we had been shocked to learn our three-year-old son, J.J., had a nickel-sized mass in his left lung. About a year before, he had complained of a tummy ache so Marsha took him to the doctor. The doctors thought J.J. probably had the flu that was going around, but just to be safe they did an x-ray to look for intestinal blockages.

Later the same day, the doctor called Marsha to deliver the results of the x-ray. J.J.'s intestines looked fine, which wasn't a surprise because he had already begun feeling better. Before ending the conversation, the doctor mentioned almost casually, "By the way, there was a weird spot near the top of the scan where we weren't even looking—in his lung. It was probably just where his shirt bunched up, though. I wouldn't worry about it."

"But J.J. wasn't wearing a shirt when we did the x-ray," Marsha told her.

"Oh. Then you need to bring him in right away," the doctor said.

About eleven months before Marsha's birthday, after a barrage of tests, the oncologists had recommended a "wait and see" plan. They were cautiously optimistic it was benign and wanted to monitor the mass carefully over time. If it was truly benign then it would probably just be reabsorbed by J.J.'s body. This would be evident on the next scan when the mass was smaller. The reason I was anxious on this particular weekend was because J.J.'s follow up scan was a few days after. I had also been feeling a bit out of sorts myself.

Earlier in the week, I had been in a rush after briefing a flight and was hurriedly trying to step out of the building to my aircraft. Before every flight, we always conduct a briefing to align all the pilots on the day's mission to our plan for action. After we complete the briefing, as a group we go to the operations desk to obtain our aircraft tail numbers. Next, we stop by the life support section to "get dressed." We each don a G-suit to keep us conscious when we endure excessive G-forces and a harness to connect to the aircraft's ejection seat, and grab our helmets.

There's one last thing all the pilots do before we go to fly—hit the bathroom. On my way to the bathroom, I was cornered in the hallway by a squadron mate with a question for me. I watched the other pilots file out of the bathroom past us on their way to their jets, and I needed to hurry to catch up with them. I went into the bathroom to pee—of course observing the appropriate man spacing rules between myself and the other pilots at the row of urinals. As I zipped up and flushed, I vaguely thought the last guy at my spot must have had a bloody nose or something and spit in the urinal. There was blood in the water. No time to think about that, I had a mission to fly. Out the door I went.

I had almost forgotten about the incident until the evening of Marsha's birthday. On our way out of the house for dinner at her favorite Mexican restaurant, I made a quick pit stop in the bathroom by our front door. I caught my breath as I started to pee. It was bright red. I immediately realized it was not another pilot's blood I saw in the urinal earlier in the week.

What is happening to my son and me?

A few days later, I stared at my flight surgeon as he informed me, "Bad news, bud. I think you might have kidney stones." Dr. Tom "Coke" Kolkebeck was a flight surgeon in our base clinic. I had known him for about a year, and he flew in the back seat of the T-38 with me from time to time.

Every flying squadron has a flight surgeon, a military doctor specifically assigned to the squadron. To ensure these doctors truly understand the unique physiological challenges pilots endure in the cockpit, they are required to fly a few missions with us each month. It is a perk flight surgeons relish.

Many flight docs have hundreds of hours of backseat time in fighter-type aircraft and are well acclimated to fighter culture. Pilots even give their flight docs call signs, sometimes irreverent ones like TAC (Turn and Cough). I don't remember how Coke got his call sign, but it was the only name I knew him by. The flight docs were part of our community, which meant they could be the picture of discipline one moment and the equivalent of our immature frat brother the next.

"Kidney stones? *Ugh*. What do I do to get rid of them?" I asked. I had heard horrible stories about kidney stones, and I had a vision of a spiky little rock making its way through my body.

"Nothing. Wait to pee them out. In the meantime, you pee in this coffee filter-looking thing to catch the stones," he said, smiling wryly as the switch flipped from impeccable professional to frat brother. "Look on the bright side, Thor, you can make a charm bracelet for Marsha with the stone once it's out."

"Gross. You're hilarious. At least we have a diagnosis. I'm guessing this is why I've been having the pain in my abdomen for the past nine months every time I fly." It was more of a question than a statement. I had been experiencing a minor pain in my lower right side near my pelvis when I pulled Gs over the better part of a year. It wasn't significant pain—about a two on a pain scale of one to ten—but it stuck around long enough for me to be concerned and mention it to the various flight docs. They all told me it was probably from "working out too hard" or some other minor inflammation. Those answers didn't satisfy me anymore. The pain had been around too long.

Coke resumed his serious professional demeanor once again. "No, I'm not a hundred percent sure this diagnosis will be the final one. These symptoms are unusual, and they shouldn't have lasted so long. I want to send you to a specialist to be sure."

As I was about the leave his office with my new coffee filter pee-catcher in hand, Coke stopped me. "How's J.J.?" he asked, concerned.

"We'll know this week. His tests are on Friday," I told him. I wondered if he could tell how anxious I was about that.

Bad News

January 29, 2010, was officially one of the worst days of my life. I flew that morning, but probably shouldn't have. I was distracted the entire mission. In the afternoon we would finally see if the nickel-sized mass in J.J.'s lung had shrunken as projected. I kept thinking about how big a nickel was in a little three-year-old body. I was terrified to think it could possibly get bigger—or worse, the diagnosis it would imply. *Cancer. In his lungs.* I forced the thought out of my mind.

One of my friends in the squadron had a three-year-old boy with cancer. He and I had talked about his son, Alan, during the previous summer. I told him about the mass we had discovered in J.J.'s lung and his expression changed to a look that said he knew all too well what horrors potentially followed this news. He proceeded to tell me the heart-wrenching story of his little boy's battle and confided his son was really struggling. I truly appreciated his frankness, but knowing his experience further terrified me.

Some of my anxiety dissipated once my family was in the car for the drive to the military hospital. J.J. was his usual chatterbox self, full of energy and little-boy mischief. He mostly wanted to talk about Superman, his favorite character, and the Christopher Reeve version of the movie that pretty much never left our DVD player. He alternated between prattling on about superhero powers and picking on his one-year-old brother, Jace, in the car seat next to him. I smiled and rolled my eyes as J.J. belted out a particularly loud version of the *Superman* theme song.

This kid's lungs are fine.

My nervousness began to return as we arrived at the hospital and walked through the maze of corridors to find the location for J.J.'s appointment. We checked in and were told it would probably be about an hour wait. After we sat down, I noticed the urology department was right across the hall. The specialist Coke wanted me to see was in there. Might as well try to kill two birds with one stone and talk to him while we were here. I thought about how great it would feel for both J.J. and me to get some good news on the medical front and put both our issues to bed. I kissed J.J. and told my family I would be back in a few minutes.

Dr. Weston was the head of the urology department. It turns out he was Coke's classmate and friend at the Air Force Academy, and Coke had already filled him in on the details of my symptoms.

"I'm not convinced it's a hutch bladder or kidney stones, Joel." He didn't use call signs, since he wasn't a flight surgeon. "I'd like to take a peek inside your bladder to see if we can get a more definitive answer."

"Okay," I said. "A peek ... like a scan? An x-ray?"

"No, I'd like to insert a camera inside you that we can move around with a remote control and get a clear look at your bladder."

I started to realize what he meant, though I hoped I was wrong. "So ... this camera that somehow gets into my bladder, do I swallow it?"

"Nope. Guess again," he said with the hint of a smile. Maybe he had been a flight surgeon after all.

Twenty minutes later, I had a probe inside my bladder and a white-knuckled grip on the steel guardrails of the hospital bed. Dr. Weston told me when I relaxed it would not be so uncomfortable. I wondered if any of his patients ever believed that.

He used a tiny joystick like an Xbox controller to maneuver the camera around my bladder. We both watched a screen displaying the camera's vantage point. If I hadn't been so focused on finding my happy place I might have found the experience intriguing. The camera showed me things I had only heard about in anatomy class. The exam went on uneventfully for several minutes, which felt like an eternity, and then Dr. Weston saw something that made him lean toward the screen.

"*Hmmmm*," he said. It was a long drawn-out sound, uttered

with grave concern. I didn't need medical training to diagnose the sound. All was not as it should be. We both stared at the screen.

This view of my bladder reminded me of the inside of a balloon. It appeared to be in perfect spherical condition everywhere except one place, where it looked like someone was poking a finger into the balloon from the other side. Whatever was pushing on my bladder from the other side was doing so with enough force to begin tearing it on the inside.

"I'll be right back," Dr. Weston said. He left me alone in the room. With a probe still in my bladder.

About a minute later Dr. Weston returned, and I think he must have brought every person in the clinic with him. They crowded around the screen and Dr. Weston continued working the joystick to see the anomaly from every angle. They were talking quickly now, but no one spoke to me.

"Could a hernia do that? Push against his bladder that hard?"

"It has to be a mass. Something is there that's not supposed to be."

"That's huge. What could it be? If it's a tumor it's certainly in a strange place. Can't be. Not at his age. How old are you?"

At this last question they all stopped talking and looked at me. It was the first time anyone had acknowledged me since they entered the room. I was naked from the waist down, had a probe sticking out of my penis, and there was a team of men and women watching *The Thor Bladder Show* on a small television screen.

Is this for real?

But all I said was, "I'm thirty-three."

They went back to ignoring me and discussing what they were seeing on the screen for a few more minutes. They sounded almost excited about this new medical discovery. Meanwhile, I was terrified and getting a little pissed off at their insensitivity. I knew what "mass" meant, I heard them say tumor, and I didn't hear much else that sounded like it would be okay. In fact, a kidney stone diagnosis sounded fantastic.

We finally finished the exam and I dressed in a state of total shock. I had come in with a little bit of pain and now I was the most interesting patient in the clinic for all the wrong reasons. J.J. was undergoing his own tests next door. I prayed silently that his were going better than mine.

I entered Dr. Weston's office and saw him sitting at his desk talking to several people who had been in the exam room. They stopped talking when I walked in.

"Joel, there's a mass pushing on your bladder from the outside and we don't know what it is. It could be benign, and there's a chance it's cancer, but either way I think it should come out." I had heard a rumor doctors were trained not to say the c-word unless there was great concern. They didn't want to scare patients unnecessarily by bringing up cancer too early in a diagnosis. I felt dizzy, sweaty, and cold.

"It needs to come out? Like surgery? Cancer?" I asked.

"We don't know if it's cancer, but it's one of the things that's still on the table. And yes, it needs to come out. As soon as possible," Dr. Weston said.

I left the office in a daze and saw Marsha and the kids walking toward me from the CT scan room on the other side of the hall. How would I tell her everything that just happened to me? A million things were spinning through my mind.

We have a vacation planned for this weekend, and there's no way that can happen now. I have to have immediate surgery. Somehow, I've got to tell her I might have cancer.

But then I saw the look on her face and only one thing mattered.

"How's J.J.?" I asked. "Did the mass shrink?" I already knew the answer.

"No," she said. I could tell she was fighting back tears. "It's gotten bigger. It's about the size of a quarter now."

The room spun. This wasn't happening. "I've got something to tell you too," I said. "Let's go to the car."

The next seventy-two hours were a complete blur. I was numb from the combination of adrenaline and surreal disbelief in what had transpired.

First I had an ultrasound scan and then saw what was pushing on my bladder from the outside. There on the screen was a bright white mass. The ultrasound technician froze the picture from her console and used her mouse to draw an outline around the intruder in my abdomen.

"It's about the size of a racquetball," she said without looking away from the screen. My tumor had already graduated out of coin sizes.

Back in his office to interpret the results again, Dr. Weston tried to reassure me. "We still don't know what it is, Joel. It's a mass, but that doesn't mean it's cancer. There are all sorts of different types of things that appear inside our bodies and many times we never even know they are there."

Our family ate at The Cheesecake Factory the next day. Well … Marsha, Jace, and J.J. ate at The Cheesecake Factory. I had to force myself to eat the little bit of food I had stomached over the past few days. I picked at the chicken madeira on my plate—my favorite—and looked around the restaurant.

This is bullshit. We take care of ourselves in my family: I am in the gym constantly, J.J. is the picture of good health to any outsider. *What's happening to us?* I glanced over at J.J. as he happily ate his chicken fingers. I'm thankful he doesn't know what's going on.

The next step for me was a CT scan. The docs were still trying to figure out what was growing inside me. I sat in the waiting room with four other patients, and at one point a woman around thirty years old was wheeled into the room with us. She was hunched over in a wheelchair clutching her thighs. Her eyes were closed, and she had an expression of immense concentration. She was only in the waiting room for a few minutes before she was wheeled in to get a scan before everyone else.

"What's wrong with her?" I whispered to the tech who was with me.

"She's got kidney stones and she's in terrible pain," the tech answered quietly.

Well there's a bit of irony, I thought. She had my original diagnosis. Even with my situation, I didn't envy her. She looked miserable.

The scans didn't tell us much. The docs got a clearer picture of what the mass looked like, but they kept telling me they wouldn't know the nature of the mass until the surgery allowed them to see inside my abdomen. I asked Dr. Weston what was still on the table and he rattled off a list of cancers and a few benign things he hadn't ruled out.

I tried to be optimistic. I kept reminding myself: *I'm young, I'm in shape, and I will fight whatever it is with all my strength.*

I spent the next few days looking up all the possible diagnoses Dr. Weston mentioned. It wasn't good. It was scary.

In my research, I quickly skimmed through the description of each type of cancer I might have and then stopped on the survivability rate. The highest survivability rate I saw was only about 60 percent. Of all the different cancers I might have, my best-case scenario was still only 60 percent. And that was after chemo, radiation, and a host of other horrible treatments.

I tried to suppress a wave of terror and disbelief, and kept reminding myself it was still possible for the mass to be benign. But the possibility was seeming less and less likely. My doctors seemed to hold out hope I had some harmless malady, but I wondered if they were being honest.

We scheduled my surgery for February 10.

Coke called me from a medical conference he was attending in California. "What's the latest?" he asked. "Any word on what it might be?"

I told him about the many different diagnoses on the table. "What do you think, Coke?" I asked, hoping for some support.

"Thor ... if it's a cancerous tumor the size of a racquetball, and it's pressing on your bladder so hard you're peeing blood. Well, it's not good." I could tell he was picking his words carefully, as if there was a gentle way to deliver this type of news.

One night, when we were going to bed, Marsha said a prayer, asking God to grant us peace in our trial. She finished with, "I pray that you help us to rest in your plan."

"Does he know what he's doing to us right now?" I almost spat out the words. I was angry, and it was the first time I had ever openly questioned God. I felt ashamed I broke so quickly.

"Don't say that, Joel," she said quietly.

I watched the ceiling fan spin for hours as the night dragged into Sunday morning.

We went to church, and after the service we approached the pastor to let him know what our family was facing and to ask him to pray for us.

As I described our situation, he looked more and more concerned. "Joel, that's terrible," he said. "And you are having surgery this week? J.J. too?"

"My surgery is Wednesday, and we are still waiting to find out the next steps for J.J." I replied.

"What's the prognosis look like for you? If you have cancer?"

"Well, not real good. All the cancers I could be facing have a pretty low survivability rate. At least according to the almighty internet," I told him.

For a second, he stared at me with his mouth open, wondering how to respond, I suppose. I'd seen the same reaction many times over the previous few days. Then he composed himself and prayed while holding hands with my family, "May God grant you the courage, faith, and peace to accept his plan," he said with his head bowed. I was struck by the similarity between his prayer and Marsha's the night before.

My family and I thanked him and began to walk away. He discreetly grabbed my elbow to stop me for a moment. He pulled me closer to talk to me privately. "Joel, sometimes it is our job to show the world how a Christian dies. I hope that is not your burden right now but know God will be with you through this trial no matter what," he whispered.

That was his guidance? It might be my turn to die like a Christian? I know he meant well, but I needed more. I wanted reassurance I would be all right and my son would be okay.

My parents came from their home in Olympia, Washington, to be with me during the surgery and to help out with the boys. I could tell they were anxious for me.

Our air force family got wind of our situation and began lining up to help out as well. The military community is truly incredible about supporting their own in times of need. My commander's wife set up a meal rotation plan to have hot dinners brought to our house every night following the surgery. They do this same thing every time someone has a new baby or faces tough times. The most recent example I saw was for a pilot called Vapor.

Vapor's wife had been diagnosed with cancer, and then found out she was pregnant. To protect the baby developing inside her, she made a courageous decision not to continue chemo treatments. She gave birth to a beautiful baby girl, and for a few days everything was fine. But things changed in a matter of hours; the young mother went into a coma and died. We were terrified by this tragedy, and now it seemed we were experiencing one of our own.

God will be with you.

I kept hearing our pastor's words in my head. They were meant to be comforting, and although I kept praying, I didn't feel a connection to God. Spiritually, I felt very alone. And even as I tried to wrap my mind around my own craziness, there was no relief from the terror I felt for my son.

Surgeries

The air force surgeon who was to perform J.J.'s procedure introduced herself quickly with a slight smile and held up a notebook to dive right into J.J.'s situation.

"So it looks like there is a mass in his left lung, and it occupies a large portion of the upper lobe. My game plan is to remove the entire large lobe. I can't just extract the mass itself because it's embedded in the lobe tissue."

She paged through J.J.'s notes as she explained her plan in a matter-of-fact tone.

Marsha and I weren't surprised to hear about having to remove the entire lobe through this aggressive surgery approach. Previous doctors had told us it would be tough to remove the mass alone, though I had held out hope they were wrong.

"Okay," I said to the doctor. "We had been warned we may not be able to remove the tumor by itself. Do we have any idea if it's cancerous or not?"

"No, we don't. But we need to plan for the worst and remove the entire lobe. Let's schedule the surgery for a few weeks from today." She slapped her notebook closed, got up, and started walking toward the door. "One of the nurses will be by to determine an available date," she said without looking back.

"Wait!" I called after her as she tried to make a quick exit. "I've got questions!"

That was an understatement. I had about a hundred more

questions. We had been talking with her for less than five minutes, during which she told us she planned to remove most of my son's left lung.

"Why are we waiting for surgery? I'm having tumor surgery in a couple days, and my doctors had tried to schedule it even sooner. And what will J.J. be like afterward, with little more than one lung to breathe with and live with for the rest of his life?"

She sighed and stopped in the doorway, one foot in the room, one foot out. "We don't know if this is cancer, Major Neeb, and based on its slow growth we can afford to wait. And I'm not sure what his condition will be like afterward. You'll have to ask other doctors about that, I just do the surgery."

I couldn't believe it. She was annoyed with me! She was going to take away almost half my son's breathing capacity. Plus, he might be facing a cancer battle, and my questions were an inconvenience to her? She paused for another second in the doorway and gave me a look, plainly conveying she had more important places to be.

I stared at her incredulously. She wheeled around and disappeared down the hallway. I tried to keep calm in front of Marsha, but inside I was fuming. I didn't want to trust my son's life to this woman. Unfortunately, this doctor didn't offer many options.

We went upstairs in the same hospital to meet my surgeon, Dr. Cartwell. With his wire-rimmed glasses, he reminded me of Egon from *Ghostbusters*.

"Major Neeb, we're going to be removing the tumor and everything else it's touching. That means we will probably have to remove part of your bladder, some intestines, and maybe even a portion of your liver."

He droned on, rattling off the host of organs I might soon be missing portions of as if he were reciting his grocery list.

"I don't understand," I said. "If you can just remove the tumor, why do you have to take parts of all those other organs?"

The thought of these doctors hacking away at my insides made me nauseous.

"We don't know if it is cancer, but we need to assume it is. If we just take out the tumor we run the risk of leaving cancer to grow on anything the tumor was in contact with."

So there it was. Not only am I going to have the tumor removed, but now I'm going to have multiple organs sliced and diced. I left the hospital and called Coke on my way home to get his medical perspective.

"Yeah, Thor, that's standard practice," Coke told me. "They're going to try to get clean margins, which means they cut beyond the potential cancer and remove some of the healthy tissue. This increases their chances of getting out all the cancer cells."

"Well this is definitely more than I bargained for. I thought this would be a pretty minor surgery, like an appendectomy," I said.

"No, bud, this is going to be bigger than that. I don't think they'll have to cut you up too much to get it out, but they will have to look around." He paused and continued with a note of sarcasm, "But if you wake up with a zipper scar from your sternum to your nuts, you'll know they did a lot of exploring in there!"

"I'm not in the joking mood, Coke. I'm scared."

"I know, bro. Just trying to lighten you up. The surgery will go fine."

Forty-eight hours later, we were preparing for my surgery, scheduled for the following day. My lower abdomen had been hurting all day long, so the surgery could not come fast enough. I did not know if it was my mind playing tricks on me or not, but since I got the news I might have cancer, the pain had ratcheted up from a two out of ten to about a seven.

Right before bed, I went to the bathroom to pee. It was bright red, and I thought I saw tissue come out. The pain made me squeeze my eyes shut and moan. This wasn't my mind playing tricks on me.

I called Dr. Selman, one of the doctors who would be helping during surgery the next day. "I'm getting much worse!" I told her. "I'm in a lot of pain, and I'm really seeing a lot of blood when I pee now."

"Joel, there's not much we can do tonight, and your symptoms are to be expected. We could get the team together and do emergency surgery, but I don't like to start cutting without a full night's rest and a proper briefing before we start. Can you hang in there until the morning?" She sounded genuinely concerned and sympathetic in her response.

"Yeah, I guess I don't have a choice. I will see you in the morning."

"Joel, it's going to feel a lot better to have the tumor out of there. You'll see," she told me.

I finally fell asleep around three in the morning. I woke up to the alarm at five in the middle of a dream.

The hospital the next morning was a blur of activity. My surgery was the first of the day. They told me it would take about four hours, and I should be out by early afternoon. They pushed my gurney into pre-op to hook me up to IVs and other medical monitoring devices. Dr. Cartwell came in the room to talk to me.

"So do you have any questions before we get started?" he asked in his monotone voice.

"Nope, not really. You explained the procedure pretty well for me the other day."

He started to get up to leave and I stopped him. I did have one question. "Do you think during surgery we will be able to tell quickly whether or not I have cancer? I mean, if it's not cancer, will you do anything differently?"

"Oh, it's definitely cancer," he said matter-of-factly.

I stared at him in shocked silence for a moment. "It's definitely cancer? What do you mean? We talked about the potential for it to be some other benign condition. You said yourself we wouldn't know until surgery." I felt dizzy.

"Yeah, we did a blood test a few days ago and the results came back last night. If the tumor markers in your blood are above 3.0 it indicates the presence of cancer. Your tumor markers came back at 36.0."

What was he talking about? There is some kind of magic blood test to tell whether or not I have cancer? Doctors had been saying all along they didn't know—couldn't know—what the diagnosis would be until they got me open. And now I hear a blood test has given us all the answers?

"Will I need chemotherapy? Radiation? I have cancer?" I spit and stammered.

"You will most likely need some treatments on the other side of the surgery, but I don't have anything to do with that. Well, I better go get ready."

And he left me with that devastating news.

I was about to be wheeled back to my family for a few minutes to say our goodbyes before surgery. They were already terrified. I just couldn't give them this last bit of news. I wouldn't steal their hope. I put on a brave face and feigned confidence.

"Hi Mom, Dad. Hi Marsha. Almost time," I said, smiling.

"Yup, and you are going to do great," Mom said. "And they are going to find a benign tumor, and it will be out, and you'll be back on your feet in no time."

"Yeah, sure. I hope so," I said.

"I know so! You hang in there and this will soon be over," Marsha said. They were being so brave.

I wanted to tell them. To say that Dr. Cartwell just dropped a bomb on me five minutes before surgery and through a magic blood test confirmed it's not a benign tumor, but cancer. And not just cancer, but cancer registering a 36.0 on the cancer meter.

I faked one more smile and the nurses began to wheel me down the hallway toward the operating room. On the way, my mom walked quickly alongside my bed and gave me a kiss and said, "It will be fine! Love you!" Then Marsha bent over the bed and did the same thing. Not to be outdone, Mom leaned over the bed to give me a kiss again and said, "You got this, Joel!" Upon seeing this new gauntlet thrown down, Marsha leaned over the bed again, kissed me, and said, "Love you, babe!" She looked up at my mom with what appeared to be a smirk. They were fighting over who would get to say goodbye to me last!

Even the nurse pushing my bed was amused. "Okay, ladies, he's had enough loving. We need to take him into the OR now." This was exactly the levity I needed at a time like this. My spirits were definitely lifted. Possibly because my anesthesiologist had just given me a dose of some wonderful chemical mood enhancer.

Mom and Marsha were left outside the OR door, and I was wheeled into the ultra-bright light of the operating room.

"You ready for this, Joel?" It was the anesthesiologist. He looked like a cool guy with close facial hair and a skull do-rag on his head.

"Sure am. Thanks for the shot." I really was feeling better already. *Cancer? What cancer?*

"Can we say a prayer before we get started? Is that okay?" I asked. The anesthesiologist shrugged and said, "Sure."

I locked hands with him and asked God to guard and guide Dr. Cartwell's knife during surgery. I asked for the courage to accept God's plan for me. I could be a little more pious with the drugs kicking in.

Dr. Cartwell came in with his mask on. The anesthesiologist did something to my IV and asked me to count back from ten.

"Ten, nine, eight, seven ..." and then nothing.

When the surgery was over, I felt pain even before I was

awake. My lower stomach muscles were spasming, jumping, and twitching, and each movement felt like it was tearing me apart. My body jerked on the bed with each new wave of spasms. I could feel Marsha holding my hand, but I couldn't open my eyes to see her.

"Joel? Joel? You with us?" said a nurse, in a louder than normal voice. I managed a grunt in response.

"You're out of surgery and in recovery. The surgery took longer than expected and there were some complications, but soon you will be able to see your family."

In a faraway place I heard "complications" and groaned. "It … hurts. So bad," I said meekly.

"Get him a pain block! Now!" the voice came from the direction of my side and had authority.

I felt my hand squeezed again.

"Thor, don't worry, bro, I've got a pain block coming now to totally stop what you're going through. They should have done one earlier." The voice belonged to Coke. He was the one holding my hand, not Marsha.

"You did great, buddy. There were some issues, but everything went great." I was glad he was there.

Once the anesthesiologist hooked me up to the nerve block it was like I hadn't had surgery. I didn't fully understand how it worked, but it sounded like they basically short-circuited my nervous system on both sides of my abdomen, so I couldn't feel the surgery trauma. I could have taken a punch to the gut and I probably wouldn't even notice. I don't remember much after I came to in the recovery room. When I woke up the next morning Marsha was at my side.

Dr. Cartwell came by to give me a report.

"The surgery went well, Joel, but it took a lot longer than expected. You were back there with us for about eight hours," he said. "I found the tumor pretty quickly. It was a little bit bigger than a racquetball, and it was squished flat against the other or-gans in the area. I removed the tumor and about ten inches of your intestines. Then Dr. Weston stepped in and removed about 25 percent of your bladder. We looked around your insides and took out about twenty-five lymph nodes too. We take those to see if the disease has spread."

I think I caught an ever-so-slight pause before he said the word "disease."

"So do you think it was cancer?" I asked. Marsha was sitting next to me, and I still hadn't told her about the news Dr. Cartwell had delivered right before surgery.

"Actually, I'm not sure. We will have to wait until pathology is done analyzing the tumor." He paused. "Your appendix looked really abnormal, though. I removed it too. If there was cancer, it may have come from there. Because of the ... bizarre ... appear-ance of your appendix, Dr. Weston came back in and removed a bit more of your bladder too. That's what took so long."

I was elated. So the infamous cancer blood test might be wrong! And if it was cancer, it might just be in my appendix, which sounded about as threatening as having cancer in my pin-ky toe.

"That's great!" I said. "And if the cancer was in my appendix, perfect! Who needs an appendix, right? Problem solved!"

This was the first piece of good news I had gotten in what felt like a long time. I was due.

"Well, we'll just have to wait and see," Dr. Cartwell didn't appear to share my enthusiasm, but then again, this guy could look depressed at a carnival.

I stopped him as he got up to leave to ask him one more question. That morning I had sheepishly peeked under my cov-ers to see if I had the infamous "sternum to nuts" zipper scar Coke had warned me about. But when I looked the only thing I could see were bandages across my entire abdomen, so there was no telling. "How big was the incision you made for the surgery?"

He considered the question for a moment. Then he closed his left hand around his right wrist and slid the closed hand all the way to the bottom of his forearm. He removed his left hand from around his forearm and showed me the distance between his thumb and middle finger.

"About that big," he said.

Great. So apparently, old Doc Cartwell had been elbow-deep in my abdomen. There was a visual I could have done without.

A week later, I was allowed to leave the hospital. It had been a week of many highs and surprisingly few lows. We were still waiting on pathology to come back with the results of the tumor analysis, so I was able to just focus on healing from my surgery. Each day we celebrated another milestone. Day 1 after surgery, I was able to get out of bed and walk around my room. By Day 2, I was doing laps around the floor of the hospital. On Day 3, I slowly began to re-introduce liquids back into my body as my digestive system healed, and just before I left the hospital I ate solid food again for the first time. It felt great to see the progress I was making. I really enjoyed the time with Marsha too. It had been such a whirlwind of activity the past few weeks, and I appreciated the mandatory downtime in the hospital bed.

When I left the hospital, Dr. Cartwell told me he would contact me as soon as he knew my official diagnosis.

The call came three days after I got home, and the doctor got right down to business.

"Joel, it appears that my hunch was unfortunately correct. Pathology came back with the results of the tumor analysis. You've got stage III mucinous adenocarcinoma of the appendix. It's appendix cancer."

There it was. It was shocking to finally hear I had cancer, but I was hopeful to hear it was in an organ as useless as my appendix. Though stage III sounded pretty scary.

"But you got it out, right? And it's just cancer that starts in your appendix, so it can't be too bad, right?"

"Appendix cancer is extremely rare and extremely serious. We checked the lymph nodes we had removed, and three of the twenty-four tested positive for cancer, which means it's spreading," he paused for a moment. "You're not going to like this next part. I have to go back in through my original incision and remove about half of your intestines."

"What? I thought you got it all out? Why would you have to remove half of my intestines?" Between the bomb he dropped on me with the cancer blood test and this new piece of information, I was really beginning to despise talking with this guy.

"It's a preventative procedure, Joel. There will be some ... lifestyle changes ... if we do this."

"Doc, this is blowing me away. I did research on appendix cancer and I couldn't find anything about going back in and removing half the patient's intestines."

"Well, I can be convinced not to do this procedure," he said slowly. Why was he suddenly backpedaling? Did I need this life-altering procedure or not?

"You can be convinced not to do a procedure to remove half of my intestines just because I started asking you questions about it? What's going on here, Doc? How many of these cases have you treated?"

I already knew the answer.

"Actually, I think you're the first case ever in the air force," he admitted.

"Well, Doc, you're not cutting your teeth on me. I want to go to a doctor who specializes in this," I said with conviction.

"I can support that."

It was the first thing he'd said that made sense in the conversation. He sounded a little relieved.

I hung up the phone and immediately called Coke.

"It's cancer, Coke. Stage III. My appendix. Mucinous adeno-carcinoma."

He sighed and was quiet for a moment. "Well, I guess I'm happy it's not stage IV," he finally said.

"That's what I thought too," I said. "Dr. Cartwell said it's pretty serious, and it has already spread to my lymph nodes. I'm still glad it was in my appendix and not colon cancer or stomach cancer or any one of the other terrible cancers I had read about and was dreading."

"Yeah ..." He didn't sound as encouraged. "I do have some good news for you, Thor. You know the surgeon who's supposed to do J.J.'s surgery?"

"Yeah, of course."

"I put in a referral for you to find another doctor. Pick out any one you like in Texas. But do it quick before she gets wind of this and raises a stink."

"You rock, Coke!" Coke to the rescue once again. I was so relieved—there was no way we could have trusted J.J.'s life to her.

I enjoyed this good news for a moment and then got somber again. "Well, I'm going to go research my cancer and find out what I'm up against." We said our goodbyes and hung up.

I got on the computer to learn about my cancer. I quickly found a website dedicated to mucinous adenocarcinoma and skimmed the page. As I read, my hands started to shake, and I couldn't catch my breath. It sounded more horrible than I imagined. Over the next few days, I researched further, hoping to find some semblance of hope. Every page said the same thing. The survival rates for mucinous adenocarcinoma in the abdomen were very low. It's a cancer that spreads to neighboring organs by contact. The tumor secretes a material called mucin, which sends cancer cells everywhere throughout the abdomen.

I imagined my racquetball sized tumor, and everything it must have touched in my abdomen. No way the doctors could have removed all the tissue it was in contact with. Even if they did, I learned it could still spread to my abdominal wall, and from there it could go everywhere. My abdomen would continue to fill up with mucin until my digestive organs were crowded out; and when my digestive system stopped functioning, I would slowly starve to death.

As horrible as that sounded, I was also learning the treatment might be worse than the disease. The only surgical approach moderately effective for mucinous adenocarcinoma was a procedure dubbed the "mother of all surgeries" by some cancer patients. I found a layman's description of the procedure online and read it in utter disbelief. The details included an incision from sternum to pelvis; removal of gall bladder, spleen, parts of both large and small intestine, and the lining of the abdominal wall; removing the outer layer of any remaining organs with a scraping tool; and finally, filling the abdominal cavity with a hot chemotherapy solution and leaving it for about ninety minutes.

This can't be a real medical procedure. This is from a horror movie. The surgeon removes as many organs as possible, leaving the patient with the bare minimum to stay alive, and then grates the outer surface of the remaining organs away with something like a lemon zester? Then they add a bucket of scalding hot chemotherapy soup and let it sit in there for an hour and a half? This is a joke.

But it wasn't. Each new web page I clicked only confirmed the horrors of the cancer and its treatment. Even with the procedure, survivability was still very low.

I spent many nights lying awake reflecting on my life and my family. My five-year survivability rate was so low I assumed I wouldn't make it until then. *But if I could just survive those five years.* I envisioned holding out until 2015. J.J. would be eight, and Jace would be six. J.J. would probably remember some good times with me, but Jace would most likely only have a vague memory of a sickly dad in his childhood. Those would be tough years for Marsha taking care of me. I prayed for sleep to come and push the thoughts away.

Some people with terminal diseases say the moment they wake up in the morning is their favorite part of the day. In the delirious space between dreams and reality, they no longer have cancer, and for a brief time everything is as it should be. They live for just one fleeting, daily glimpse into a life that no longer exists.

This was not true for me. Waking up became the hardest part of my day. Every morning in the seconds before I was fully lucid, I had a momentary wave of relief that everything was all just a dream. I don't have cancer. J.J. is not going to have most of a lung removed. I'm a strapping fighter pilot, and my family is the picture of good health. It was all just a nightmare.

And then slowly, cruelly, reality crept back in. The details are not those of a dream: An appendix cancer specialist in San Diego said at best I had a fifty-fifty shot of making it through this. We met J.J.'s surgeon. Every morning it was the same. I was not waking up from a nightmare. I was waking up to one.

I spent my days in a state of delirium from stress and lack of sleep. Not wanting to be left alone with my thoughts, I followed Marsha around the house like a puppy. I looked for any distractions to allow my mind to focus on something else, even for a moment.

Every Friday night, J.J. and I watched a movie together, usually *The Lion King*. In the past, when we had watched it, I fast-forwarded past the part where Simba's father dies. I thought it was too much for a little boy to handle.

One night, I let the whole movie play through, and J.J. saw Mufasa's true fate. After the scene ended, J.J. asked, "What happened? Why did the daddy die?" I hoped he couldn't see my tears in the glow of the television light. Later that night, I stood in J.J.'s doorway and watched him sleep, wondering if one or both of us would be gone soon.

I pushed the thought away angrily.

It doesn't matter. None of this is real. This is all just a dream. It's a nightmare. Why can't I wake up?

J.J.'s surgery was scheduled for February 23. We talked to him about the procedure in the days leading up to the event. Marsha and I sat him down and told him he had an "owie" in his body and a doctor had to cut it out.

It definitely helped that I had just had surgery myself. I was recovering quickly, and J.J. got to see me back on my feet again, at least most of the time. He was still concerned about the whole "cutting" piece of this process.

"But you don't let me touch knives. Cutting hurts," he said.

"I know, bud, but this doctor is trained to use the knife to make a small cut, and take out the owie through the cut." I had a brief vision of Dr. Cartwell illustrating the size of the incision he made and forced it out of my thoughts.

J.J. had one stipulation for the surgery. If the doctor was going to cut him with a knife, J.J. insisted he was wearing his Superman costume to the hospital. Marsha and I smiled at each other. The Superman costume made regular appearances around our house. J.J. would put it on at least once a week and wear it for the entire day. In J.J.'s eyes, there was only one problem with the costume. In the Superman movies he loved, the hero always wore red bikini briefs on the outside of his blue pants. J.J.'s costume didn't come with those red briefs. He solved the problem by wearing his underwear on the outside of the costume.

Of course, he wore the full outfit to the hospital, topped with a pair of Underoos. Marsha and I laughed uncontrollably as he darted between people with his arms outstretched, cape billowing behind him and his underwear on the outside of his pants.

By the time we got to surgery prep, we were no longer laughing. This had been much easier when I was the patient. They made J.J. take off his Superman costume and put on a gown. He was very concerned when they put in the IV but determined not to cry. He looked so little in the big hospital bed. I wanted to switch places with my son so badly.

"It's time," the anesthesiologist told us.

"J.J., buddy, it's time. Are you ready, big guy?"

Smile. Keep it together. Don't let him see you losing it.

"Yup." He looked up at us.

The anesthesiologist leaned in and whispered to Marsha and me. "Now, when I administer the general anesthesia, he may have a negative reaction."

"What do you mean?" I asked.

"Well, usually everything is fine, but once in a while a child will panic as the anesthesia sets in. It can be a bit confusing, and I don't want him to fall off the table. Dad, I'm going to need you to hold him down." The anesthesiologist told me.

Hold him down?

"Okay," I said uneasily, and then turned toward my son. "J.J., bud, we're going to give you some special juice now, okay? It's like Superman juice. It is going to make you sleep and help the doctor to take out the owie."

"Okay," J.J. wasn't concerned at all.

The anesthesiologist began to deliver the sedative, and I gently put my arms around J.J. to be ready in case he panicked. Sure enough, as soon as the chemical wound its way through the IV cord and into my son, his arms began to jerk upward against me.

"Easy, buddy! Everything's okay!" I said.

Why couldn't anything be simple anymore?

"Joel, let him go!" Marsha said. "Look! He's ... flying."

Marsha saw what I didn't. J.J. wasn't flailing in panic. As the Superman juice entered his system, he was raising his arms to fly. He drifted off to sleep with a faint smile of delight on his face.

J.J.'s surgery went well, but the following days were tough. I visited him in ICU as much as I could, but because of my recent surgery and compromised immune system, the hospital staff didn't want me spending much time there. Part of me was glad to be shooed out of the ICU. I couldn't bear to see my son in pain. When he wasn't in pain, he was wheezing for air.

This shouldn't be happening to us.

Marsha was a rock. She stayed by his side from the moment he got out of surgery. There wasn't one second when she didn't display confidence and support for him. She rubbed his forehead when he moaned and cried out in pain. She helped him do exercises the doctors gave him to strengthen his remaining lung capacity. I was humbled by the depth of her strength.

After J.J. came home, he recovered quickly—faster than I did. Together, we walked laps around the kitchen, which the doctors told us would help our wounds heal. We had to wait for the pathology to find out whether J.J.'s mass was cancerous or not, but his surgeon told us he was betting it was not.

After J.J.'s surgery, I spent some time trying to figure out next steps for my cancer. We found a hospital for me to go to in Houston. The University of Texas MD Anderson Cancer Center, one of the best cancer treatment centers in the world, has a specialist for mucinous adenocarcinoma.

When we went to Houston in early March for my first visit, I felt blessed to know my doctor was not only a specialist, but world-renowned in the field. We lived only a few hours' drive from the hospital, so I could conveniently go there for all my care. *So why did I have this horrible feeling of dread and anxiety?*

I didn't say a word to Marsha on the long drive. Several times I had trouble catching my breath.

When we arrived at the hospital, Marsha dropped me off at

the front and went to park the car. I stared up at the enormous building, many stories high, with scores of people entering and leaving.

As I walked toward the entrance, I glanced up at the all the windows, and suddenly I realized why I was so anxious.

This is the place where I will die.

I stared at the walls of glass going up toward the sky and wondered in which room I would take my final breath.

I started walking slower, then I stopped, overcome. I squeezed my eyes shut and hot tears streamed out.

With my eyes closed I faced heaven.

Where are you God? Because I'm going through this alone! Do you even care? Fix this! We don't deserve this! Where are you when we need you?

I was angry, and it felt good to release those emotions. I had been pretending to be strong for so long. When I finally opened my eyes again, I saw her. She was being wheeled into the hospital by her parents. She was maybe nine years old. Her skin was pale and loose, and her body was gaunt. She didn't have any hair, and she wasn't wearing a hat to hide it. I couldn't see her mouth because it was covered by a surgical mask. But I did see her eyes.

She had striking, beautiful blue eyes, and the moment I noticed her our eyes locked onto one another. I continued staring at her as she whisked past me, and she turned her head to hold my gaze. She met my stare unashamedly, but in her eyes, I also saw something else.

Her fear. In just a few moments of eye contact I saw her struggle, the weight of her disease, and death, and everything else a nine-year-old shouldn't have to carry. I desperately wanted to help her, because I knew I was stronger. I had thirty-three blessed years to fall back on. I had a beautiful wife and two sons who love me. She might not live to be a teenager.

A moment later, she disappeared down a hallway, and I was

left standing outside the entrance to the hospital by myself again.

All my self-pity was gone, replaced by a worse feeling.

I'm sorry. I've been so selfish. I'm so sorry, God. Thank you. Help her, Lord. Not me. Help her.

I wiped away my tears and made a promise to never feel sorry for myself again. I steeled my nerves and entered the hospital with fresh determination to meet whatever comes.

No Surrender

MD Anderson seemed like a cancer treatment assembly line. Hundreds of patients roamed the hallways, congregating in enormous waiting rooms. Yet we were seen quickly and then moved on to the next appointment. It was extremely efficient and a completely different experience than the one I'd had at military hospitals.

After several administrative appointments, I found myself on the seventh floor at the gastrointestinal clinic. I was ushered into a small patient room and introduced to the man who would become my primary cancer doctor. I had already read about the renowned Dr. Mansfield, but this was the first time I'd seen him. He was tall and unassuming, friendly and patient with all my questions.

"Did you read the report from my air force docs? What did you think of their proposal to go back in and remove half my intestines?" I asked. This was the question I had been wondering about for days.

"Well, that wouldn't have been my approach," he said. "That's an option, but it's an aggressive one, and it's a little outdated. We have more effective surgical procedures these days."

"Like the mother of all surgeries?" I asked.

He gave me a faint smile.

"So it sounds like you have been on the appendix cancer support forums. We don't call it the mother of all surgeries around here, but it is definitely a beast. I've performed about a hundred of them."

"When do you think I will have to do mine? After chemo or before?" I asked. I had pretty much resigned myself to facing the horrific surgery.

"Well, let's wait to see if we need to do that. You don't have any signs of cancer right now."

I was shocked. "But I thought the surgery was preventative? Don't I need the surgery to help me beat this?" I had not read about appendix cancer patients who didn't have this procedure.

"There's nothing to beat right now. You don't have any signs of cancer." I think he could tell by my expression I was still confused. "Joel, let me tell you about my job. My job is to balance the length of your life with the quality of your life. Sometimes it's necessary to sacrifice one for the other. If we do the ... mother of all surgeries, you will definitely decrease your quality of life. You might not increase the length of your life. Now I don't want to get your hopes up. You will most likely have to have the surgery at some point. But let's wait until we're convinced we are going to increase the length of your life."

"Makes sense," I had to admit I was glad to hear we weren't scheduling the mother of all surgeries—or any surgery—anytime soon. "So we do chemo?"

"I think it's the best approach. You've got stage IV, which means it's moved into other organs, and it's also in a lymph node so ..."

"Wait. You said stage IV. It's stage III," I corrected him.

He opened his folder and paged through the paperwork. "No, it says stage IV in my notes. And by the way, it doesn't really matter. There's a fine line between stage III and IV with this type of cancer, and it doesn't make much of a difference in survival rates."

"But the air force medical staff said it was stage III," I said in disbelief.

"Well, my staff said it was stage IV, and I trust them more," he said. I trusted them more too.

"Let me show you how far the cancer's traveled," he said and quickly sketched out an anatomical diagram to show me where the cancerous lymph node had been retrieved. It was on the opposite side of my abdomen from where my appendix was. My mind reeled as I considered the distance the cancer had already spread in my body.

I waved my hand at the drawing and looked away.

"Okay, okay, I believe you," I said. I was quiet for a moment. I had one more question left. The toughest one. "Do you think I can beat this, Doc?"

He paused and looked at me with understanding before speaking.

"Joel, we're all going to die," he said.

It reminded me of my pastor's words.

Sometimes it's our job to show the world how a Christian dies.

Dr. Mansfield continued. "I don't know if this is what's going to kill you or not, but I do know we have a medical plan to either beat it or slow it down."

That would have to be enough for now.

I finished my appointments and took my family back home to San Antonio with a new plan. We would do the chemo at the air force hospital near our home, and I would return to Dr. Mansfield and MD Anderson every few months for checkups. Much of the anxiety I had felt before the trip was gone now. It felt good to have a plan, but there was another reason I wasn't constantly focused on my own battle anymore.

I kept thinking about the girl at the entrance to the hospital, picturing the look in her eyes. The youthful boldness of her stare mixed with the fear of what waited for her inside that building.

I prayed for her often. For the first time in a while I wasn't consumed with thoughts of my own fate. I only hoped seeing that girl wasn't a glimpse into J.J.'s future.

Days after my visit to MD Anderson, we received unbelievable news. The pathology department finally came back with their analysis of the mass from J.J.'s lung, and it wasn't cancer! He still had a long recovery ahead of him, but he didn't have cancer. The mass was precancerous, so it likely would have become cancer in the future. The surgery to remove it probably saved his life.

We were ecstatic. We took J.J. to his favorite restaurant and picked up dinner to go. For the first time in a very long time, I wasn't worried about my son. As we ate at our kitchen table, no one was thinking about health issues. We were just a happy family once more.

That night, I quietly opened the door to J.J.'s room while he slept. I knelt on the floor near his bed and thanked God for my healthy son.

The following days were strange. Over the weekend, I received a call from Nuke, a pilot friend who was part of the Thunderbirds team at the time. Back in January, I had applied to join the team.

"Thor, it's Nuke!" I had known Nuke since my first assignment in the air force, and he was always full of energy and confidence, a typical Thunderbird. "How's it going? We're going through applications to join the team, and I saw yours. But I heard you might be sick. What's the story?"

"Hi, bud. You're not going to believe this. I still don't really believe it. I've got cancer."

I hated telling people that. It sounded so feeble and so final.

There was silence on the phone line.

"What? Are you serious? Oh man, I can't believe it, I'm so

sorry." I could tell he was genuinely concerned. "Thor, I hate to ask this, but I'd really like to see you on the team, and, well … is it something you think you'll recover from soon?"

"No, Nuke. It's not," I said.

I heard him sigh. "I'm so sorry, Thor."

"Yeah … Hey, I'll get better and apply again next year, Nuke." I didn't believe that, but the conversation was getting depressing.

"Yeah, for sure. Wow. Thor, I don't know if I should tell you this, but … I really think you were going to make the team."

"Thanks, Nuke," I had dreamed of being a Thunderbirds pilot since I threw my hat in the air at the Air Force Academy graduation. Before my hat hit the ground, the Thunderbirds flew over in a perfect formation five hundred feet above us.

I barely reacted to the news they had been strongly considering me for the team. That felt like someone else's dream now.

A few days later, I got another call, this time from a company called Afterburner. Afterburner is a consulting group that hires former fighter pilots and special operators to help corporations adopt combat-proven leadership methodology.

The chief operating officer at Afterburner called to tell me their CEO, Jim "Murph" Murphy, was in San Antonio and wanted to meet me. I had sent in my resume a few months earlier, but since I hadn't heard back from them, I didn't think anything would come of the opportunity.

For a moment, I thought about saying right then that I had cancer, and there really wasn't a point in anyone taking the time to meet with me, but I just couldn't give up on that dream too. I made plans to meet Murph, who was also a former fighter pilot. He was scheduled to speak at a large event downtown, so I made plans to meet him there.

I put on my best suit—no small feat considering I still had a catheter and a urine bag strapped to my leg. I pulled into the giant parking garage at the Henry B. Gonzalez Center. For a brief moment, I felt a twinge of excitement at the prospect of joining this team. I could still do this—even with cancer.

Then my phone rang.

It was someone from the military treatment facility where I would receive my chemotherapy, informing me I had to come in immediately to have the port installed for receiving my chemotherapy. Apparently, the surgeon who would perform the procedure was going on leave the following day. The port had to be installed right away to avoid delaying my chemotherapy treatments for another month, said the voice on the phone.

"I have to drive myself in for surgery. Right now. And this is the earliest you could tell me?"

I sighed and shook my head in disbelief and perpetual disappointment in our government medical system. "I'm coming over."

I hung up the phone. Who was I kidding? There would be no Afterburner in my future, just like I would never fly for the Thunderbirds. I needed to accept the fact that the rest of my life would consist of medical appointments and healthcare. I was not feeling sorry for myself. This was just the way it was going to be from now on. We got the incredible news that J.J. didn't have cancer, but the same news would most likely never come for me.

I called Murph to tell him I wouldn't be joining him for his presentation. He didn't answer so I left a message on his voicemail: "This is Joel Neeb. Thor. I was on my way to meet you, but ... you're not going to believe this. I have cancer. I really wanted to shake your hand and tell you I still wanted to be on your team, but I think I've got to take care of this first. My doctors just called, and I have to go back to the hospital for a procedure."

I knew Murph would think I was crazy when he heard that message. Or feel sorry for me. I wasn't sure which I preferred less.

The chemo port procedure went smoothly. The port was essentially a gateway to my jugular vein, allowing my medical care providers to draw blood and administer medications more easily. My chemotherapy schedule consisted of twelve doses, delivered one at a time, every other week.

Cancer relies on rapid cell division to grow and take over an area, and chemo is a weapon to slow down or stop the growth. Healthy cells need to divide every day as well, meaning my hair would stop growing, my immune system would slow, and my healthy blood count plummet.

The morning of my first treatment, the chemo room was full of patients receiving their treatment, most with battle wounds of recent surgery. They were all smiling. In the middle of their darkest hours, in the fight for their lives, these people somehow found the capacity to make the decision to be joyful. I was humbled to be in their presence and found myself meekly smiling as well.

The first day, I sat down next to an older couple. The woman leaned over to me and asked, "First time?"

"Is it that obvious?" I chuckled.

She smiled. "You just look too healthy to have had this poison in you before."

The nurse came over. "Ready?"

Do I have a choice?

I thought of the little girl at MD Anderson and the countless rounds of chemo she probably had in her short life.

"Let's do this," I said.

A thumbtack-sized pin was inserted into my port—okay, that hurt—and was connected to a machine next to me. The nurse pushed a few buttons on the machine and it whirred to life. Chemotherapy fluid snaked down the IV line and into my body.

It took about four hours in the chemo room to receive my treatment. They disconnected me from the large chemo machine then connected me to a smaller one about the size of a football. They sent me home with this tiny version. My chemo treatment would be spaced out over a few days in order to minimize some of the negative side effects of the medicine. The machine would continue to deliver more chemo for the next forty-eight hours while I was at home. It made goofy noises every five minutes or so when it delivered another dose of chemo.

In case I wasn't humbled enough yet by the golf ball-sized port bump in my chest and the pee bag strapped to my leg, I also had to carry around a chemo fanny pack.

I really hadn't experienced too many side effects yet. I felt a little flu-like and tired, but that could have just been my imagination. There was one side effect I was particularly interested in investigating.

My doctors told me one of the strangest effects of my chemo would be cold aversion. All cold objects would feel many degrees colder than they actually were. I was warned to bundle up in a scarf and gloves for my trip home from the chemo treatment. So far, things hadn't felt any colder. I decided to test it out a little further.

I opened the door to the refrigerator and put my hand inside. Nothing. Felt like a fridge. I touched the cold milk jug. Still nothing. I smiled as I considered that I must be immune to this particular side effect. That only happened to the other guys. After all, cancer or no cancer, I was still a fit fighter pilot. Chemo wasn't so bad.

I poured a glass of ice water and took a long drink. Before I could react, my hand involuntarily opened, and the glass crashed to the floor. When I swallowed the cold water, it felt like ice daggers inside my throat. I gasped and waited for the pain to subside.

I finally caught my breath and looked around for a towel to clean up the mess I had made. "Well, that was stupid," I said aloud to the empty room. My little chemo fanny pack whirred and buzzed as if in agreement.

Throughout the next few weeks, I endured several rounds of

chemo. I began to adjust to the rhythm of the treatments and ensuing symptoms. The first day after treatment I generally did not feel any side effects. A few days later the chemo really kicked in and made me feel like I had a horrible case of the flu. My cold aversion went into full force and I stayed away from both the fridge and freezer. Food tasted different, but it didn't really matter, because I had lost my appetite.

A few days after each treatment, I returned my chemo fanny pack and waited for the symptoms to subside. Around a week after each treatment I came out of what my family had begun to call my "cave"—the bedroom upstairs where I hibernated as I recovered from each treatment. My pillow collected a nice pile of hair, and the hair that did grow on my head came in with a silver tint.

Finally, the day arrived when the doctors removed my catheter and my pee bag. My bladder had finally healed enough to function normally. This was not only a huge milestone but a significant psychological victory for me. I hated that damn thing.

There was one more thing I needed to do. Ever since seeing the little girl at MD Anderson, I had made a commitment to skip self-pity and stand up to my cancer. I needed to go outside and run.

I had been extremely active before getting cancer, but then was laid up in a bed for a few months. I had finally healed enough from my surgery to get a little exercise. It was a beautiful day, so I grabbed my running shoes, my headphones, and our dog, Chloe, and hit the streets.

It hurt. My surgery scar hurt. My lungs hurt. With each step, my feet and hands tingled from nerve damage, another side effect of the chemotherapy. I had to mentally focus to stay coordinated in my stride. But I was running. I had recaptured a small part of my healthy life. I was out of breath by the end of my street, but I continued anyway. In my headphones, the band Survivor belted out the chorus I had listened to thousands of times before during my workouts. Those same words held new meaning:

In the warrior's code, there's no surrender. Though his body says stop, his spirit cries, "Never!"

I developed a very different outlook on my life.

Every time I found myself starting to return down a path of self-pity, I thought about the girl I saw at MD Anderson. If she could find the strength to face her trials, I certainly could. My new perspective allowed me to take a larger picture of my situation, and not just focus on my immediate fear of the cancer battle.

I felt my faith and relationship with God strengthening as well. My prayers became deeply personal and much more intimate. I found an undeniable peace as I grew to trust God in a way I had never allowed myself to before.

I found myself focusing on what I could do for my family and my community before I got too sick. I created video messages to my kids for future birthdays, holidays, graduations, weddings. It pained me deeply to think I would miss it all, but the pain was less raw than it had been in the past. I knew God was in control, and he wasn't biting his nails wondering what would happen.

I knew he would either lead me back into good health, or he would lead me through this into eternity.

Another month passed, and I received another round of chemo. I had been getting to know the people in the chemo room fairly well. Most of them were older than me, and they could talk about their cancer as if we were discussing the weather.

After we passed through small talk, we always returned to one topic—what we were going to do when we were healthy again. We discussed our future healthy lives in exquisite detail.

"When I can taste food again, I'm going to eat whatever I want," one patient said.

"Not me!" said another, "I'm going to eat healthy food for the rest of my life. It's taken cancer for me to realize food is fuel."

"I'm going to move to be closer to my family," another proclaimed wistfully.

A determined man in his midforties declared, "I'm going to take the trip I've always wanted to take, and I'm going to start my own business."

No one dared address what we knew was true: some of us would never return to good health.

I was in the middle of a conversation with the man sitting next to me when his doctor interrupted us.

"Charles, we're not going to be doing chemotherapy today," the doctor said to him. He looked serious.

"Why not?" Charles asked.

The doctor glanced at me as if wondering whether or not to continue the conversation there. "Your blood numbers show the chemo has weakened your body. And your tumor markers have been unaffected. It doesn't look like chemo is helping, Charles. We need to try another approach. Let's go back to my office."

The room was silent as Charles gathered his things and left. Everyone knew there were no other treatment options. Charles's hope of returning to good health had come to an end.

I closed my eyes and said a prayer for Charles and his family. Before we were interrupted, he had just finished telling me what he would do when he got healthy. "I'm going to the World Cup this summer in Spain. It's been a lifelong dream." I wondered if he would live that long.

Over the next several weeks, I felt compelled to share my story. I had learned so much from my experience, so much I wished I had known before cancer struck: To appreciate the simple things. Not sweat the small stuff. Live for today. To unapologetically go after my dreams.

Cheesy Hallmark greetings represented the desperate pleas I wished I had understood when I was healthy. I wanted to put an exclamation point on these trite messages with my story. I wanted to use my pain and progress to help others.

The autumn before my cancer outbreak, I had participated in a youth outreach event with about thirty kids. I contacted the same group to see if we could put together another event.

I called the organizer and explained, "I've got cancer, and I want to do another outreach event. I have a lot I'd like to share with the kids."

"Absolutely," said Robin, the coordinator for these youth outreach opportunities. "How many kids would you like there?"

"As many as possible. Hundreds. I have reserved a theater. Let's fill it," I told her.

Not long after that conversation, seven hundred kids poured out of more than a dozen buses and piled into the theater at the air force base. They were from several different schools. As they filed into their seats, I saw a few of them give me a quizzical look. By now, my hair was really thinning and what little remained had a silver tint. My skin looked slightly yellow from liver damage due to the chemo.

Once the kids were seated, I began to tell my story. I opened with stories of J.J.'s surgery, about my cancer battle, about how my friends from the air force had stepped up to take care of me, and how I was most likely dying from cancer.

I saw a young girl in the front row begin to cry for me as I described my situation. She looked about the same age as the girl from MD Anderson. I fought back my own tears as I shared the lessons I had learned over the past several months.

Flying Again

Doctors expect tumor marker numbers to fluctuate over the course of treatment, but generally an upward trend means the treatment is ineffective. My numbers had gradually dipped to 2.6, down from 7.0 just after surgery. But then they bumped up again to 3.6, above the 3.0 threshold indicating the presence of cancer.

My doctor suggested waiting a few weeks, then repeating the blood test.

An air force nurse called with the results. "Good morning, Joel, just wanted to give you the results of your tumor marker test." I felt my heart rate and breath quicken.

"They're at 4.2," she said cheerily, oblivious to the implication of the number she just read to me. I closed my eyes and dropped to a knee.

It's back. The cancer's returned. It probably never left. I knew it would come back, but I thought I had more time.

With this realization, I phoned my medical team at MD Anderson. A physician's assistant named Lan answered the phone.

"Lan, this is Joel Neeb, a patient of Dr. Mansfield. I just got a tumor marker test back and the number's risen for the second time. It's at 4.2 and stabilized above the 3.0 threshold."

She knew right away what that meant. "Joel, we need to get you in here for some tests." Her voice sounded grave.

"Okay," I paused before I continued. "Lan, couldn't this just be a false positive? Does it have to be cancer?"

"Oh, Joel ..." her compassion was evident in her voice. "Tumor markers are the primary way for us to know if cancer has returned. If they are on the rise, there is little else it could be. I'm sorry. You hang in there."

A few weeks later, we celebrated J.J.'s birthday. It was also the day I went back to MD Anderson for an update on my cancer. We began the day with a cookie cake for J.J. in a hotel in downtown Houston. I wished him happy birthday and closed my eyes as I held him and said goodbye. My appointment was scheduled for 11:00 a.m. My emotions were a mixture of elation for my healthy son and anxiety for the cancer update I would soon receive. I sat by myself in the waiting room on the seventh floor. Waiting was always the most difficult part. I concentrated on controlling my breathing.

Be strong!

I gritted my teeth in resolve. Whatever the news, I would continue fighting until the bitter end.

"Bring it on," I whispered. In a few moments, when I received the inevitable news that cancer had returned and had spread, I would not cry. I would not despair. In fact, I would say, "Praise God." He will either lead me from this into good health or through this into eternity.

Sometimes it's our job to show the world how a Christian dies.

My pastor's words echoed in my ears. What I had once considered horrific advice had become my anthem.

"Joel." I heard Lan's voice from across the room. My determination was set, and I would face this. I gathered my things and entered her office.

As the door shut behind us she immediately began talking. "Joel, I don't believe it, but your tumor markers have gone down! They're lower than ever. Your scans are totally clear!"

My mouth fell open in stunned disbelief. I managed to weakly say, "Praise God!" while the tears streamed down my face.

As soon as I got to the hospital lobby on the first floor I called Marsha to give her the incredible news. We were both ecstatic. The fight was by no means over, but at least we had a few more months of good health.

As I waited for Marsha to arrive to take me home, I noticed a man standing next to me talking on his phone. His wife was sitting in a chair near his side. She was expressionless and stared far away. I could not help but overhear the words in his phone conversation:

"Hi, hon. Yeah, it's not good news. Mom's cancer has returned, and it's spread into other organs … I know. We're going to see the doctor again tomorrow and talk about next steps. I don't know what we'll do."

I could not bear to listen to it anymore and I walked away. My heart ached for this family who got the news I was expecting.

When I returned home, I laced up my shoes and took Chloe out for another run. The side effects from chemo were getting worse. My lung capacity was diminished, and I was forced to take big gulps of air. My sweat felt cold and clammy, as if I were working out with a hangover.

With each step on the pavement, I felt shockwaves of pain from the neuropathy, the damaged nerves, sending electric signals up and down my legs.

But the pain felt good. It reminded me I was still alive. I was still in the fight.

I *get* to fight.

I dug in and picked up the pace.

Over the next few years, I made running a part of my daily ritual. I reflected on the people who had battled cancer beside me. They fought just as hard as I did. My dear friend from college Clinton Land lost his battle to brain cancer and would never hold his young daughter again or watch her grow up. My mother-in-law Shelley cared for my kids while I received chemo treatments and then found out she had stage IV cancer. She died within eighteen months. ESPN commentator Stuart Scott inspired me and many others as he battled like a warrior until the last moment against the same cancer I was diagnosed with.

We fought together, and every one of us hoped desperately for the day when we would return to good health. During the fight, the hope was just out of reach. The hope was so tantalizing that a mere glimpse into our old lives, even if just in a dream, was like a drug. But the dream wasn't real, and somehow, of all these warriors, only I remained.

I had not fought any harder than they did or wanted to live

more than them. Yet I had a new day to look forward to, free from chemo treatments or the two-ton weight of cancer that accompanied every waking moment.

I had another chance they did not receive, and I thought much about what I should do with my chance.

Should I go back to living my life the same way as before cancer? No. I should be different in some way, but how?

First I had to fight hard to get back inside the cockpit of a jet. When I approached my flight surgeon the first time about returning to flying jets, he was dismissive.

"The recurrence rate is too high for your cancer. We're just not out of the woods yet, and we don't know how your body will respond while you're pulling Gs and flying upside down by yourself in a multimillion-dollar aircraft. We can't accept the risk."

So I spent a year "playing pilot"—going to meetings with the other pilots, providing flight academics to the students—but still grounded and restricted from strapping on a jet and getting airborne.

I focused on my physical recovery. I got back in the gym, ran, lifted weights. The words of my doctors always motivated me to do one more rep.

Remember, this cancer will probably come back.

If it did come back, my body would be ready.

I used my fitness to get back my flight qualification too. I prepared for the air force physical test, which included pushups, sit-ups, waist measurement, and a mile-and-a-half run.

The test hurt. When I took it, my body hadn't fully recovered from the chemo treatments and surgeries. But the pain spurred me on; the pain and the memory of the little girl from MD Anderson, my inspiration to always do more.

I got the maximum score on the test. Only half of one percent of all the healthy officers achieve this score. It would serve as my first real, public victory following my cancer diagnosis.

Nobody saw all the private victories required to get there, but I knew it started with willing myself to put one foot in front of the other and run when I was still in chemo.

After the fitness test, I went straight to my flight doc's office, still in my sweaty athletic clothes. I took a paper copy of my test results and threw it on his desk.

"Still think my body's not ready for the cockpit? I just aced your physical fitness test."

I was back in the cockpit the next week.

My pilot hands came back quickly. Within a few weeks I was nimbly executing the same maneuvers I had before cancer, and my body felt great handling G-forces and acrobatic maneuvers like I had done before cancer.

Physically, I felt the same in the cockpit, but I knew I was different. I had been changed by my brush with death.

The epiphany came when I was flying several thousand feet above the ground, upside down, just a few feet away from another aircraft. It was a maneuver I had flown and instructed thousands of times in my career. The formation position is called "close trail," and it's exactly what it sounds like. One aircraft is positioned just behind another, but below the turbulent jet wash coming out of the engines of the plane in front. The following aircraft maintains position behind the lead aircraft, mimicking every maneuver as the lead plane rolls inverted and does barrel rolls just a few feet ahead.

It's disconcerting for many new students. It feels like tailgating another car way too closely, and all the other driver has to do is tap the brakes to cause a collision. This is obviously not a concern in the sky, as the lead aircraft is going to maintain speed throughout the maneuver and doesn't really have brakes anyway. But it still makes many students sweaty and anxious as they struggle to maintain position.

On this particular day, the lead aircraft turned upside down, and I followed, as I had countless times before. While inverted I happened to look up (which was down to the ground since we were upside down), and I saw the aftermath of a major car accident, thousands of feet below me on the freeway I would use to take home later that day. Traffic was backed up for miles.

Oh great. It's going to take forever to get home today.

I was flying a jet hundreds of miles an hour upside down next to another aircraft, and I was concerned about the traffic on the commute home. It dawned me that I was firmly planted in my comfort zone.

I could do this in my sleep.

When I was twenty-two and learning to fly, every time I flew a jet I was outside my comfort zone. The first time I was alone and upside down in an aircraft, roaring across the skies of Mississippi, I thought my heart was going to beat out of my chest. I'll never forget looking up and contemplating that the only thing separating me from a three-mile fall to earth was a thin seat belt and a half-inch of canopy.

But the day of the traffic jam, I knew that few things surprised me in the cockpit anymore. Flying had become a job. It was an incredible chapter in my life. But I didn't want it to be the book. It was time to find new adventures.

I didn't survive cancer to stay in my comfort zone—even one in the clouds. I didn't want my new life to become just like my old one.

I decided right then I would look for another job, one that both challenged and exhilarated me.

New Adventures

Leaving the military fifteen years into a career is not a smart thing to do, according to conventional wisdom. Under the benefit system at the time, if I retired at twenty years I would get retirement pay and benefits for the rest of my life. If I got out early, I walked away without the retirement pay and fewer health benefits.

But I was still pretty sure cancer was going to come back, and I didn't know if I would have much more than six years to live. My family could use the guaranteed monthly income, but we weren't paupers, and the retirement benefits certainly wouldn't make my family rich if I died.

I decided to take the risk. I walked away from my military experience to pursue a corporate career. While still on active duty, I applied to business schools and began my studies through the University of Texas.

Meanwhile, I had been learning more about Afterburner. I thought the business model of employing stellar military officers as business consultants was brilliant. As a fighter pilot, I always believed the people in my squadron could accomplish just about anything they set their minds to. I watched young leaders in their midtwenties orchestrate a formation of aircraft in training to prosecute an attack while traveling faster than the speed of sound. Surely a group like this could do wonders for corporate America.

But business school taught me there was a chasm between my military experience and the corporate world. I had been talking about airplanes, barrel rolls, and missiles for the past fifteen years, not OpEx and EBITDA.

I committed to reading a book a week to close the gap between my business school peers and me. I may not have shown up to class with a decade of experience reading income statements, but I had something to offer business teams. I had operated in highly complex, dynamic, high-stakes environments my entire career. This skill set would help me lead teams through challenging corporate scenarios. My bias toward action and ability to quickly gather data and act decisively stood out as much as my lack of business knowledge did in the beginning. I had found a new calling, and it was to help corporations lead and succeed through chaos, much like I did in the sky with my fighter pilot brethren.

Two months after graduating business school, in October 2014, I left active duty. I said goodbye to flying supersonic aircraft to accept a full-time consultant position with Afterburner.

At each of my follow-up medical appointments, the oncologist would say, "Good news, you don't have cancer!" and then follow it up with, "But I want to you to know it will most likely come back."

I had a brutal disease, and of those I knew who were also facing this disease, I was one of the few who continued to get good reports from the doctors. I lived in a constant state of waiting for the axe to fall.

Cancer survival rates are reported in one-, five-, and ten-year increments. With my type of cancer and stage, there was a 15 percent five-year survival rate. In other words, I had an 85 percent chance to be dead at the five-year point, and if I weren't dead, I would probably be at death's door.

Instead, as 2015 and my five-year cancer anniversary approached, I felt fantastic. I thought of all the cancer patients I had met over the years who weren't as fortunate. I had to do something to commemorate this anniversary, raise awareness for this type of cancer, and really put the exclamation point at the end of my cancer battle. But what could I do?

I had a few friends who were competing in Ironman triathlons. It sounded crazy: swim 2.4 miles, bike 112 miles, and run a full marathon, 26.2 miles, at the end. This was totally outside my comfort zone. I could barely swim far enough to retrieve my water ski when it fell off in the lake. The last bike I owned said "Huffy" on the side, and I had never run a marathon, much less run one after a rigorous ocean swim and hundred-mile bike ride.

The thought of competing in an Ironman terrified me. For one thing, I had a fear of being in open water. At the beginning of every Ironman race, thousands of contestants enter the water and start swimming simultaneously at the start gun. Triathletes call this swim "the washing machine" because of the turbulence of so many people swimming together in a confined space. It's like being part of an anxious school of tightly packed fish panicked by a predator. And that's just the first challenge of the day.

It sounded terrifying, which made the Ironman the perfect way to challenge my fears and commemorate five years of freedom from cancer.

While I trained, I thought of all the people who told me I would never make it to that point.

"We all know how long Joel will last at the Air Force Academy," a high school teacher said to me in front of a classroom full of students my senior year. "He'll be kicked out within the first year."

"You won't make it six months in the air force," my military training advisor told me at the Air Force Academy.

"You'll never be a fighter pilot," my flight commander told me in pilot training.

"Have you ever looked at the mortality rate for your cancer?" asked one doctor when I asked if I would ever fly again.

Sadly, the biggest naysayers were close friends, who had been questioning my goals for some time.

Why are you going to business school?

Why are you leaving the air force?

Why a triathlon? You've never done a marathon before. You're setting yourself up for failure.

Plenty of people told me competing in an Ironman was stupid, even risky, and wouldn't prove anything.

But I had learned long ago how to feed on negative feedback, and so I began training. All those voices rang in my head and fueled every swim practice, every run, every bike ride.

You can't, they said.

I will, I responded.

At four o'clock one morning, my alarm rang out in the darkness, waking me for another three-hour workout. I was tired. My kids hadn't seen much of me lately. My family was sacrificing as I prepared for the Ironman. That morning, in the darkness, hearing the warble of my alarm, I realized I no longer cared what the naysayers thought. I had nothing to prove to them—only to myself.

I was free from any obligation to prove those critics wrong. Their doubt spurred me into action, but I was free from those voices in my head. I knew they were wrong. I had nothing more to prove to them. I could roll back over and go to sleep with a smile on my face, knowing I didn't need to complete a race for anyone else. But I didn't go back to sleep, because I could still hear one voice.

Weak and battered from years of asking when cancer would return, it cautioned me that completing an Ironman was impossible. It whispered I still had crippling chemotherapy nerve damage in my hands and feet, and I would never complete a race like this.

This voice was the only one I had to answer. It was mine.

I vowed I would complete the race for me. I needed to finish the race to finally close the chapter of my long cancer battle.

I got out of bed with a renewed sense of purpose.

I spent hundreds of hours training for the Ironman. I trained over the winter while I traveled for work, using whatever equipment was available. In the middle of a snowstorm at a small hotel in Toronto, I worked out for four hours on a hotel stationary bicycle. Later that month I biked more than sixty miles through freezing rain and woke up the next day at 3:00 a.m. to swim two miles in an empty pool. It was arduous and terrible, but I was training for me, and every session was connected to a deep sense of purpose for this journey.

With race day only a week away, all sorts of people told me how great I was going to do:

"Don't worry about it, you got this!"

"You're going to do great!"

"This will be easy for you, Joel!"

One of my close friends from business school, Ryan Larson, sent a different message:

"Joel, I hope you suffer."

Ryan was a mixed martial arts fighter before he attended business school. He was a top-ranked competitor who knew what it was like to go up against a terrifying opponent.

"I hope you suffer. I'm so jealous of what you're about to go through! I train for years for the moment on the mat when I'm being choked out, and I have to find the strength to continue. It's in that moment I learn about myself, my boundaries, and push beyond what I was before."

Ryan couldn't have been more right.

In the moments before the race started, more than a thousand competitors gathered in the water to get ready for the swim.

A cannon explosion signaled the start of the race. The mob of competitors began to swim in unison, creating the washing machine effect I had heard about. I was kicked by the person in front of me, hit by an arm from the person at my side. The water boiled with surf and movement and frothed so hard I could only see a few inches in front of my face. I was suffering, but there was something else—I felt exhilarated. The moment I had been waiting for, that I had trained for, had arrived. The cancer battle that had almost destroyed me was symbolically ended by this effort. I had to force my lips to close around my teeth under the water because I was smiling so big.

Ryan's hope was fulfilled. I suffered, but I also endured and finished the Ironman, pushing myself beyond what I thought I was capable of. It was glorious.

I proved to myself that cancer had not stopped me.

Since my cancer diagnosis, I've become more intentional in every area of my life. I've grown closer to my family. We've had hard conversations we might not have had in a cancer-free life. I fought to get back into an air force cockpit and fly again, and then chose to leave the military career I loved to pursue another adventure in a corporate career. I climbed the ranks of my company and became the president within two years. I competed on national television as an American Ninja Warrior. Climbed Mount Kilimanjaro. Dove more than seventy-five feet below the surface of the ocean on one breath.

Along the way, I've failed more times than I can count, and certainly failed more times than all the years before cancer, possibly because I have taken more chances than I ever did before. I had played it safe in the years leading up to cancer. I was coasting on the accolades of past accomplishments, not willing to risk losing my status as an accomplished person by failing at something new. I was missing out on so many adventures, because I was more concerned about maintaining the progress I had made in my life. Cancer cured me of that fearful mentality.

My son has a raspy voice from the scar tissue in his lung. He fought hard for his own accomplishments, most notably, swimming a lap in a pool at four years old. And he did it just a few months after the surgery that took away most of his left lung. To reach his goal, he spent weeks in the water, each day swimming a little further until he could finally make it the entire length without touching the ground. He emerged from the water victorious, and his mother and I could scarcely believe he was the same boy who only months earlier struggled to breathe with each step. The video of him achieving this goal is one of my treasured possessions.

We've suffered. We've endured. But we've accomplished so much more than we ever thought possible. And we're just getting started.

Asking Why

BEFORE HIS CRASH AND EJECTION, Chris had more than 2,000 hours in fighter aircraft and had flown the same maneuver 258 times. An investigation answered some questions about how it happened, but not about why on this day circumstances converged to create catastrophe.

Joel knew the dangers of being a fighter pilot, but he didn't have any risk factors for cancer. At thirty-three years old, he was fit, ate right, worked out. Why did cancer attack his body so viciously? Why had a tumor found his young son's lung? Why did his family have to suffer through two soul-crushing health crises at the same time?

After these individual traumatic experiences, our first instinct was to ask *Why?* For many people, including both of us, healing begins with this three-letter query. While tears are still fresh, and the body still aches from the impact, both the mind and heart begin seeking a reason for the pain.

Why did this happen?

Why did it happen to me?

In a maneuver flown successfully by the Thunderbirds for fifty years, why didn't I fly it successfully today?

Why did I get one of the rarest cancers? Why did others die even though they fought so bravely in their medical battle?

Why did a drunk driver hit my car and not the one in front or the one behind?

Why was I born into an abusive family?

Why did I survive?

Resolving the many questions of a traumatic event is a crucial part of the transition to posttraumatic life. These questions can bring us, as sufferers, to a new, more deliberate approach to the future or plunge us into deep depression wrought with regret and sorrow.

Asking *Why me?* is a natural starting place to begin the healing process, but it's not where we should remain. Asking *Why?* leads to more questions and doubts—about capability, skill, attitude, personality, life—about everything. Even if all the surrounding facts and extenuating circumstances are available—and usually they are not—the answer remains elusive.

For us, asking *Why did this happen?* led to one simple answer. *It happened.*

Individually, that's all we could know. We would have to take that knowledge and move forward. That's all. Deal with the facts and learn from them. Nothing could change what happened. No way to definitively answer why tragedy struck. Those experiences became permanent chapters of our individual history, journey, and identity.

People rarely ask why good things happen. A great spouse. Healthy children. A safe drive home from work without being blindsided by an eighteen-wheeler. The good stuff just happens, often without further reflection. Only acceptance.

When painful events happen, acceptance is an important step. The journey toward healing requires it. As we grew to accept what happened, we found our paths to healing through gratitude, growth, and giving. For each of us, the questions worth asking are those that look to the future with these three concepts in mind.

Chris's outlook after his crash evolved from disbelief, anger, and sorrow to the joy of recognizing he was blessed with more life to live. Realizing many had lost their lives in military service, he moved from sorrow to gratitude for the opportunity to grow old with his wife and see his children mature into adults.

In his battle with cancer, Joel found it difficult to find reasons to be grateful. His family received blow after blow. How could they be thankful? His attitude was reset by his encounter with a young girl battling cancer. Joel's eyes were opened to what he could be thankful for. He had already been blessed with thirty-three years of life, a family, and a career he loved. That moment brought another realization for Joel: If a chance encounter could change his level of gratitude, how much more could he change it by cultivating a habit of gratefulness? From then on, Joel decided he would no longer feel sorry for himself.

We both became deliberate about being thankful, determined to find reasons for gratitude each day. Talking over breakfast with the kids in the morning, happy memories of holidays and vacations, dinner out with our wives, a few hours without anxiety.

True gratitude encompasses bad times as well as good. Both provide opportunities to learn and grow. Often the lessons learned in hard times can't be learned anywhere else.

While gratitude is finding joy in the present, growth is the pursuit of the next opportunity for the future. When we each believed death was imminent, we considered our legacies. Joel had a few years to ponder, and Chris had microseconds, but we both came to valuable conclusions that pointed forward to growth.

For both of us, growing and moving forward holds a measure of risk. Chris realized he had to overcome fear and admit his struggle with PTSD to those who loved him most. Joel decided to set goals that both challenged and scared him a little—or a lot—such as leaving the military or competing in the Ironman. We have to take risks and face fears every day to grow beyond our traumatic experiences.

When gratitude and growth begin to take hold, the next step

is giving. Giving is an expression of both gratitude and growth. Whether it's offering time, money, and abilities; sharing stories, expertise, lessons learned; or helping others who are experiencing battles of their own, giving brings us full circle, revealing even more reasons we can be grateful, and helping us grow.

Gratitude, growth, and giving are all part of our journey toward asking questions focused on the future, not the past. These perspectives give new meaning to our questions, such as *Why did I survive?* They change our tone from concern over what happened to appreciation for what comes next. Our questions take on a new tenor.

Why was I granted this gift of seeing another day?

How can I fulfill the reason I survived?

Am I on the correct path to accomplish it?

These are the questions we ponder with each sunrise and every sunset—questions that inspire us to live intentionally.

The question *What did I do to deserve this?* sums up the burning desire and the elegant mystery we work to resolve each day. Although we may never know the answer, asking the question keeps us moving forward and provides us with drive and determination to accomplish our goals.

Instead of seeking reasons for either suffering or survival, we have rediscovered our most important reasons to live.

Perspective and Purpose

IN THE FINAL MOMENTS before Chris's aircraft impacted the ground, a vision of his wife flashed before his eyes, a vision that drove his actions from that point forward. As he pulled the ejection handle and physically shed his aircraft, he also shed the identity that had defined his adult life, a separation with more force than the rocket power of the ejection seat. For nine years, Chris had enjoyed nothing more than strapping on a fighter plane and slipping the surly bonds of earth. In his most honest moments, he realized there were times he had focused too much on his career. In a microsecond, he had to decide whether his identity as a fighter pilot was worth going down with his plane and losing life with his family.

After being diagnosed with a cancer almost guaranteed to end his life, Joel spent two years reflecting on that life, taking stock of the legacy he would leave behind. As a pilot, Joel had not been driven to achieve ever higher levels of performance. He had been giving just enough effort to slide through today and get to tomorrow. He had an incredible wife and family and a dream occupation. What more could he want? After his diagnosis, he didn't regret any of his failures, though he had as many as the next man. He didn't regret anything he had done. He regretted what he hadn't done. Busy with being comfortable, he hadn't taken time to pursue a larger life. He had allowed daily minutiae to block out the big picture. He'd assumed he would always have plenty of time, but he didn't. Facing what might have been his last days on earth, he became aware of what he wanted most from whatever days remained.

Painful or traumatic experiences often clarify the essentials of life and bring priorities sharply into focus. Positive everyday moments can be equally significant. The following personal stories reminded us how a moment in an ordinary day can bring new vision to a familiar view, revealing what matters most.

Chris: View from the Sky

In 2014, my team hunkered in a small concrete bunker in Afghanistan as enemy rockets flew overhead. My body was heavy with what we called our "battle rattle" and it reminded me ever so slightly of the Gs of flying fighter aircraft. My mind drifted to a simple morning back in 1999:

With a storm bearing down on the Gulf Coast, the sky was overcast, and rain fell intermittently as I strapped into my McDonnell Douglas F-15C Eagle. After takeoff, the climb took me through rain and clouds, emerging into a beautiful sunlit sky. A quick look in my rearview mirror revealed the storm falling further behind me. Many people below were heading to work under a sky that promised a wet and dreary day, but the weather was amazingly beautiful from my office window.

As I leveled the aircraft at fifty thousand feet, I could see multiple states—from the point where Mississippi kisses Alabama in the West, to the southward curve of Florida to the east. The rain and wind of the thunderstorm that beset my morning commute from home to the base stayed below me.

My eyes followed the curvature of the earth, and as I looked across the horizon, it seemed I could almost touch the layers of the atmosphere, each with its own distinct color. I wondered what lay just outside the protective atmosphere of our planet. Even in the middle of a summer day, the sky began to darken, and stars became visible.

I reflected on the clarity of that vantage point. What we can see from the surface of our world is limited in scope, size, and distance. We usually think of what we can see at ground level as finite reality, never considering how the limitations of our location affect our perceptions of the infinite.

With the complexity of a daydream within a daydream, memories of my family and the adventures we shared over our years of military life fanned out like the states sprawled below my view from the sky.

As my thoughts drifted back to my bunker in Afghanistan, I vividly imagined the day I would fly home and embrace my family after this deployment.

The "all clear" rang through my forward operating base indicating the attack was over. As I climbed out of the confined protection of the shelter, I could not focus on anything else until I could again hear my wife's voice. With urgent steps, I returned to my bunk room and clicked the connect button on Facetime to call Terri.

Before my ejection, a view of the earth from the edge of the atmosphere was something I may have taken for granted. Reflecting on that same experience while I was deployed and far away from my family reminded me to deliberately take time to reexamine what I considered routine and be intentional in every moment of our lives.

Joel: Pressures of the Deep

Free diving is an interesting sport. It involves taking a deep breath of air and descending as deep into the water as possible on just one breath. That's all there is to it. But the mental and physical journey is so much more.

I belong to an organization for young executives, the Young

Presidents' Organization, a network for business leaders who share best practices and learn from one another. One common behavior for this group is they make a habit of facing fears on a regular basis.

About a year after I joined, some members of the group invited me to go on vacation with them. Of course, a "vacation" with this group is not sipping margaritas on the beach. No, they wanted to travel to Bonaire, an island just north of Venezuela, and learn to free dive. Why were we going free diving during one of the few vacations we would get this year?

Because we were afraid of it.

We were afraid of going without air for a prolonged period of time, afraid of drowning, afraid of the claustrophobic terror of being far beneath the surface of the water.

The group wanted to take on this challenge to face the fear. Me too.

Looking down from the surface, I saw a rope snaking downward, disappearing into an infinite blue haze. I took a deep breath and started my journey into the depths, equalizing the pressure inside my ears as the water pressed harder, ever harder, against me as I slid downward.

The increasing pressure embraced me peacefully at first, like a womb. Farther down, it weighed on me like a coffin. Against every instinct, I continued to swim straight down. What was once a blue void became a distant ocean floor coming into view. Glancing upward, I saw the last slivers of sunlight. I continued farther into the abyss, a rush of exhilaration as I explored a new world unreachable by anyone on the surface.

Then the first pang of air hunger interrupted my bliss. *Maybe I should slow my descent*, I thought. The desire to inhale grew stronger.

At the turning point, the realization hit: I have to travel the same distance back to reach the surface for one precious breath of air.

Controlling my mental state while ascending was my only option. Going too fast causes panic, expends energy, and increases the risk of blacking out before resurfacing. Going slow is not an option either. I simply had to endure to reach my goal.

This is what I enjoyed so much about free diving. I had no choice but to steel my mind and focus on making it back to the top. The little secret: I wasn't running dangerously low on oxygen when the air hunger first hit, not then. I had another minute or two before that threshold.

But I was running out of perseverance, running out of the will to power through the air hunger consuming me. I was losing the ability to persevere through the lingering sense of panic that edged its way into every fleeting thought. With every bit of strength I could muster, I kept the panic at bay.

Instead of giving into the fear as I ascended toward the breath I craved, I focused intensely on moments of peace and happiness: My children, moments in their lives my mind chose as the most poignant. My wife. My parents. Emotions from a specific wonderful memory. These flooded my mind and happily distracted me from the pain of air hunger.

In less than two minutes, my journey was over. I breached the surface and gasped a breath. But I was not focused on the mental battle, or even the air I hungrily took in. Instead I longed for the moments of tranquility and remembrance I had just experienced.

I went more than 75 feet below the surface. One of my colleagues went down past 110 feet. We learned a lot about our physical limits, but we learned more about ourselves. There were times when we felt overwhelmed by the challenge and others where we shined. But that is life, and we dove deep to discover it.

The pressure of the ocean enabled me to focus on what made me feel peaceful and fulfilled. After resurfacing, I wanted to dive

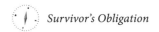

again—not for an adrenaline rush, but because my deep dive put me in touch with the beauty of my life.

Whether flying high above the earth or diving deep below the ocean, significant moments—life-threatening or not—reveal what is most valuable. This knowledge informs the decisions that shape our course.

Suffering, pain, and loss sharpen our awareness of what is essential. They lift us above the everyday and give us a wider perspective of our lives. They also put pressure on us, focusing our hearts and minds on our true sources of strength and purpose.

Decisions

SOME LIFE DECISIONS ARE EASY, between clearly good or bad options: Get a job or start a life of crime? Easy, get the job. Find a career with incredible benefits and opportunities or invest everything in the lottery? The odds favor the career.

Other decisions are not so simple: Focus on career advancement or family relationships? Career advancement offers personal gratification, and a secure income is good for the family too, right? Play it safe or take risks to follow a dream? Why risk everything on potential failure? Why live life without a dream? Safe is nice, but is it really better than sorry?

Family, income, personal fulfillment, and big dreams are not mutually exclusive. It is entirely possible to pursue more than one goal with care and deliberation. The difficult choices are the daily decisions that maintain balance between those goals. On any given day, the scales weigh heavier on one side or the other. The key is making consistent decisions, not based on the need or emotion of the moment but on deeply held values.

Military members and first responders train deliberately to proactively develop the skills to perform successfully in critical moments. They develop conditioned responses to stressful or emergency situations. They learn to act deliberately with purpose, rather than react fearfully in panic. This intense training is repetitious and exhausting, but it prepares them to maneuver safely and effectively, whether in extreme situations or on routine missions. We should be just as deliberate in our everyday lives.

The story of Chris's ejection takes many pages to tell, but it only took 25.25 seconds to unfold, from takeoff through impact. When he realized during the flight he could not complete the maneuver, his training took over. He had never ejected before, but he knew what to do. He executed each movement, decision, action, and reaction exactly as he had trained to do many times over the previous nine years of his career. He experienced no panic, no confusion, no fear. His ingrained skills focused all his decisions and actions on a single objective: survival—for himself and those watching on the ground.

Living by our values requires making daily decisions—both large and small—to conform to those values and corresponding goals. This means acting with purpose and on principle, rather than reacting out of fear, anger, or other emotions. Circumstances may allow time to think through an array of choices, or they may not. Forming good decision-making processes over time improves the quality of all decisions, even those that have to be made quickly.

The process of learning to make intentional decisions, like any training program, is not always enjoyable or easy. While training to be a fighter pilot, Joel became discouraged by the repetitive and sometimes unrewarding days of training. Flying 300 mph was not what he anticipated. It was less like the wispy cloud-chasing of his dreams and more like a constant series of tasks: check altitude, check airspeed, move the throttle to slow down or speed up, move the stick to fix altitude, look outside to avoid other traffic, answer the air traffic controller on the radio, repeat.

One day after a particularly discouraging flight, Joel was on the runway when another plane—piloted by one of his classmates—roared overhead. Joel saw the soaring jet, felt the booming sound of its engine, heard his friend's confident voice on the radio. Joel had just completed a similar flight pattern and radio transmissions. From inside Joel's cockpit, the flight felt mechanical, rote; but seeing his classmate in flight changed his perspective. From his vantage point on the ground, the results of rigorous and repetitive training were apparent and impressive.

Learning to fly is not all soaring, but soaring is the final result of hard work and training. Similarly, it can be difficult to decide in favor of deeply held values or goals, but the long-term results are rewarding. Since becoming survivors, we have retrained our thought and decision-making processes to make choices that align with what is most important in our lives. The process is demanding but worthwhile.

Before Chris's accident, he focused primarily on being a fighter pilot. He loved his family, but spending time with them was often secondary to time in the cockpit and to his military career.

Now family time is Chris's priority, and he makes daily choices to reflect this focus. Instead of making time for his family when or if his work schedule allows, Chris plans his schedule around time with his wife and children first.

Every morning after having coffee with Terri, he talks with his two youngest children, Aubree and Andy, while driving them to school. He returns to spend time with Terri in the hot tub before going on with his workday. Every evening, the family has dinner together while they discuss the events, emotions, accomplishments, or discouragements of the day. They talk about their dreams and what's important to them as a family.

For weekends and holidays, Chris often chooses to spend time at the beach, on the lake, or at home with his family. His number-one priority now is to be present for the little things, which he used to take for granted but now recognizes as the big things in life. These are small pieces in his daily life that add up to strong relationships.

Chris and Terri see the results of these choices when their

grown children, Zach and Bethany, adjust their own work schedules and plans to make family time a priority too.

Before Joel was diagnosed with cancer, he settled for mindless ways to fill time rather than seeking valuable ways to spend it. After his diagnosis, he recognized time as a precious and nonrenewable resource, and as a survivor he has become more intentional about using it. He pursues those intentions with his family. Together they keep an ongoing vision plan for their family, and each year they review it together. They talk about what adventures they want to pursue, and they set spiritual, physical, and intellectual goals individually and as a family.

When Joel competed in the Ironman Triathlon, Marsha and their sons came alongside him—sometimes to train with him, often with notes of encouragement, always with love and support. Marsha and the boys completed the last mile of the race with Joel, celebrating the victory they shared. Each member of the family identifies individual adventures, as well. At four years old, J.J. met his goal to swim a lap in the pool not long after his surgery. At twelve years old, he set a goal to run six miles. The Neeb family took up four treadmills at the local gym to train with J.J., and they were at the finish line to meet him when he met his goal. Inspired to take on her own personal challenge, Marsha competed in a regional fitness competition, winning her category.

The whole family shares a dream for new adventures, and they make plans and set goals to make their dreams come true.

Survivor's Obligation

WE AND OUR FAMILIES HAVE BEEN CHANGED by our experiences, physically and emotionally. Some changes are readily apparent, others less so.

It may not be immediately obvious that Chris turns his whole body instead of his neck to look over his shoulder. Under his business suit, he usually wears a transcutaneous electrical nerve stimulation unit to surge electricity through his back to overcome muscle damage and continual pain.

Though Joel may not look like he fought a battle with cancer, the nerves in his hands and feet are permanently damaged by chemotherapy treatments. His fingers tremble slightly as he buttons his shirt. He's prone to drop things, because his hands don't clasp properly. His feet tingle, and his damaged nerves periodically send shockwaves up his legs, particularly while he is running.

We both experience panic attacks. These are often unexpected, but their origins are no mystery. They are the psychological remnants of our battles, bubbling up when something sparks a memory. Our brains instinctively revert to the fight that's never quite over, searching for a demon that is gone but not forgotten.

Joel's son J.J. doesn't act like he's missing part of his respiratory system, but the long, jagged scars on the side of his body tell a different story: the story of a life-saving surgery, when doctors broke the cartilage between his ribs and removed part of his left lung, piece by piece.

Our wives Terri and Marsha don't reveal the emotional pain they have endured and the struggles they have overcome to support us and our families through difficult days. Both families are living satisfying and productive lives, but we have each been changed, transformed by our experiences, and determined to live in a new way.

The day before Chris's ejection, or the day before Joel's cancer diagnosis, we each would have described ourselves as content. We each had proud accomplishments both personally and professionally, a long list of victories: United States Air Force Academy grads, flight school standouts who went on to break the sound barrier and fly in combat. Two successful military officers with impeccable careers and beautiful families.

The day after our traumatic experiences, we each viewed life very differently. After surviving the unsurvivable, we each found clarity about what was most important to us, the essentials of our existence. Receiving the priceless gift of more life to live, we wanted to live differently by focusing on those essentials. In the journey to turn those realizations into reality, we discovered we had questions to answer and new decisions to make.

Acknowledging the many questions of a traumatic event is crucial to healing from it. Through gratitude, growth, and giving, we turned questions about why we experienced such painful events away from the past and toward the future. Instead of wondering why the trauma happened, we began to ask what we could do with the rest of our lives. For us, gratitude, growth, and giving transformed concern over the past into appreciation for the future.

Living for what is essential means making daily decisions that fit our values and our corresponding goals. We have learned to choose deliberately and act intentionally, rather than react to the emotions of a moment.

Every life is finite, and every life, whether long or short, is full of choices. As one of Joel's doctors reminded him, "We're all going to die." We have both chosen to invest fully in the life that comes after survival, rather than using our lives to dwell on the pain we experienced.

Survivors of accidents, illness, war, broken relationships, or other painful experiences often find that going through those experiences clarifies what is most important in life to them; but an experience doesn't have to be traumatic or painful to be life-changing. Everyday experiences and events can also bring us new perspective when we take time to reflect on them.

As far as we have come since surviving the unsurvivable, we know there is no endpoint—healing is a journey. For us and our families, each day brings new challenges and reminders of our anxieties. Yet each day also brings new opportunities and possibilities. Navigating each day requires intentionality, a compass that points us to our true north. Each day as survivors, we remember the perspective we've gained, we commit again to the purpose we've discovered, and we do our best to make decisions that keep us headed in the direction we've set for our lives.

We each resolve to fulfill our responsibility—our survivor's obligation—to live life in a new way for ourselves and our families, and in honor of those who didn't get a second chance. We choose to embrace each and every day and live intentionally.

Acknowledgments

IT IS BY GOD'S HAND we are both alive. We are thankful each day, and it is our simple hope to live up to the expectations and achievement for which our lives were permitted additional days.

To our readers, thank you for joining us on this journey. We are all survivors, and from this point forward, we ask you to join our quest to *Live Intentionally*!

From Chris

To my wife, my best friend and my partner on this journey of life, Terri: You amaze me each day. In your eyes I feel heartfelt hope, devoted faith, and transcendental love. Thank you for your strength, support, and dedication to our lives and our family. Without you, none of this would be possible.

To my children, Zachary, Bethany, Aubree Lu, and Andrew: You did not choose this military way of life, but you embraced it with grace and courage. Never forget you are the result of experiences and decisions of yesterday, and through each move, each challenge, each day we amass experience to be used in our tomorrows.

To my Thunderbirds teammates: You are the most amazing and professional military team ever assembled. Max and Terry, your dedication to the Six Load was unwavering from the time you saluted on the taxi out to the day you watched it go up in flames. Thank you to the team that pulled an all-nighter on my aircraft to replace the ejection seat just before I used it. You used your time and expertise to replace the ejection system because it simply distracted me when I flew. Without these actions, I wonder if the results would have been the same. To the person who packed my parachute, thank you for your attention to detail. A record three pilots ejected that year and parachuted to safety under your canopies.

From Joel

Writing this book meant reliving some of the most painful and beautiful periods of my life. I want to thank my wife, Marsha, and our children, J.J., Jace, and Makenna, for their unending support and devotion through the ups and downs of this journey. I am humbled to be part of this incredible team as we experience life's adventures together.

To J.J.: Your strength in the face of a terrifying ordeal inspired me to be better during my trial. Watching you struggle and finally succeed as a four-year-old—swimming a full lap with most of your lung removed—is one of my most treasured memories. This book doesn't exist without your shining example of perseverance.

To my air force family: You promised we would never go into battle alone, and you meant that in every respect. You surrounded our family with love, meals, and support at a time when we needed it most. You're truly the best of us.

Last, to God, who was always by my side, but lost in the noise until I needed you most. Thank you for the trial, for the lessons, and for the second chance.

Reader Reflection

How do the authors differentiate between survivor's guilt and survivor's obligation? What are the differences? Why is this an important distinction?

During the ejection sequence, Chris describes the temporal illusion of time moving very slowly. How could this illusion be helpful in a moment of crisis? How might it also help later when processing the trauma of crisis?

A military investigation evaluated the causes of Chris's crash. Does knowing the reasons for a traumatic event make it easier or more difficult to process?

Joel was unsatisfied with the words his pastor spoke to him after his cancer diagnosis. Later he felt differently about what his pastor said. How might time and experience change the perception of words of encouragement or advice?

Joel describes a turning point in his journey after a brief encounter with a young cancer patient. How does empathizing with another person's experience cause a shift in perspective?

Asking questions helped Chris and Joel come to terms with the traumatic events they experienced, even when they didn't have the answers. Why, in some cases, is asking questions more important than finding answers?

After a life-threatening trauma, survivors may experience changes to or questions about their spiritual faith. Joel's personal faith transformation brought him "an undeniable peace." In what ways does exploring faith impact healing? Does faith inform a sense of survivor's obligation?

Chris and Joel found healing from their traumatic experiences, in part, by choosing gratitude, growth, and giving. How are these choices related or interconnected?

Chris tells a story about finding perspective while flying at fifty thousand feet. Joel writes about free diving and the clarity he found in the pressure of being deep under the ocean. How do perspective and pressure clarify priorities and choices?

Chris was able to act almost without thinking during his ejection, making decisions and taking action based on his training. How does training affect decisions and actions in other types of intense situations?

For Joel, the hard work of flight training seemed different from inside his own aircraft compared to watching his pilot-training classmate soar across the sky. Why was it easier to see and appreciate the result of hard work and training from outside the cockpit rather than inside it?

Joel did not want to further worry his family by telling them about the cancer before his surgery. How does a desire to protect a loved one impact communication choices?

Even years after his ejection, Chris had a hard time talking with his wife about the lasting effects of the incident, including his PTSD. How might their healing have been different if they had shared their emotional journeys with each other sooner?

Chris and Joel were changed by their experiences in both negative and positive ways. How can changes that are negative, such as physical scars, play a part in creating positive change?

Throughout the process of sharing their stories to encourage others, Chris and Joel had to recall intense moments of their individual journeys. Even years after a traumatic experience, triggers or reminders—whether purposely recounted or brought on unexpectedly—can bring feelings of anxiety and fear, inducing setbacks or emotional shutdowns. In what ways can the emotional pressures caused by recalling past trauma also bring clarity and a new perspective toward progress?

Chris and Joel came to recognize healing as an ongoing process. Each established daily routines and personal goals to remind themselves of the life path that best aligns with their priorities and values. What are some other positive reminders that can serve as a personal compass to navigate each day's challenges and opportunities with purpose and intention?